BEYOND YOUR WILDEST DREAMS:
Access, Activate and Achieve Your Heart's Desires

Dr. Chuck Crisco

Beyond Your Wildest Dreams: Access, Activate, and Achieve Your Heart's Desires
By Chuck Crisco

Printed in the United States of America

ISBN-13:978-1545037287
ISBN-10:1545037280

CONTENTS

Hearts.
Heart Truth 10—Your Entire Being is Trying to Fulfill the Images in Your Heart.
Heart Truth 11—The Heart Can't Tell The Difference Between Real And Imagined.
"I Can Only Imagine" Exercise

The Power of Radical Hope: Embody the Future Now
Heart Truth 12—The Heart is the Epicenter of Emotions.
Exercise: "Your Feeler"

CONCLUSION: What Now?
Heart Truth 13—The Heart is Established by Grace through Patient Faith.

13 Core Heart Truths

Heart Truth 1—It Is a Change of Heart That Changes Things.
Therefore, instead of getting new information alone, love allows heart changes.

Heart Truth 2—The Heart Is Designed to Function in the Present Tense.
Therefore, learn to love life and peace rather than judge it.

Heart Truth 3—Your Heart Is the Conduit Between the Spirit on One Side and the Soul on the Other.
Therefore, learn to live from the glory of love within you.

Heart Truth 4—The Heart's Beliefs Form an Authority System.
Therefore when you believe God is love, it will have a ripple effect and your entire life will change.

Heart Truth 5—The Heart Is the Place from Which We Believe.
Therefore, change your focus and allow God to author new beliefs about love.

Heart Truth 6—The Will of God is Found Inside Your Heart.
Therefore, trust desires that are consistent with love.

Heart Truth 7—The Heart Is the Place of Intentions.
Therefore, grace will back up your loving intentions.

Heart Truth 8—Your Heart Is like a Thermostat… Whatever You Love Will Eventually Become Your Norm. Therefore, love life, love your desires, love your dreams.

Heart Truth 9—We Don't See with Our Eyes, We See with Our Hearts.
Therefore, to avoid only seeing what we already see we must love perceiving a new vision.

Heart Truth 10—Your Entire Being Is Trying to Fulfill the Images in Your Heart.
Therefore, impress new images of love to get new experiences of love.

Heart Truth 11—The Heart Can't Tell the Difference Between Real and Imagined.
Therefore, give your heart the images that you love of your desires.

Heart Truth 12—The Heart Is the Epicenter of Emotions.
Therefore, align your desires and emotions with love and they will be fulfilled.

Heart Truth 13—The Heart Is Established by Grace through Patience.
Therefore, in love sustain the new beliefs, feelings and images until they are fulfilled.

Introduction: The Law of Love

"How wonderful it is that nobody need wait a single moment before starting to improve the world." – Anne Frank

I sauntered out from behind the curtain as I burst out with song, *"If you want to view paradise, simply look around and view it; anything you want to, do it; wanna change the world... there's nothing to it."* It was Costume Party Sunday at the church I was pastoring where people were dressed like a hero that they admired. I was dressed as Willie Wonka, with hat, ruffles, cane, the works.

I love the scene when he brings everyone into the Chocolate Factory and they step into the world that his imagination created! I love that song because I feel it in my bones. I've learned through trial and error, ups and downs, epic failures and extraordinary victories that we really do possess the capacity to change our world beyond our wildest dreams.

I fully embraced my character and sang with all my might that day hoping to inspire others but I was not expecting to be the one inspired. One guy came in that morning wearing a shirt that was just like one of my favorite embroidered shirts. As I curiously approached him and his wife I realized that it wasn't just like my shirt. It was my shirt. The two dressed up like my wife and I because, to them, we were their heroes for being courageous enough to be ourselves.

I can't tell you how moving that was for me because it was an affirmation that the life I was choosing to pursue really was meaningful. That was a time in my life when I quit trying to fulfill other people's dreams for me and started living more authentically from my heart. It was costly but so liberating to know that my dreams were coming to the surface and I was on the right path in my journey. Everything in my life was changing and so will yours when you are willing to see your wildest dreams come true.

So many dreams of mine came true. I travel to exotic remote places in the world, write books, write blogs read by hundreds of thousands, started businesses, planted churches, speak before thousands, met famous people, encouraged others through television appearances, participated in miracles, love my friends, coached people into spiritual peace and joy and I'm connected to a beautiful family. Do you know what? I am just getting started.

What is your dream? Can you taste it? Can you see it? Do you know that it is within reach? Or maybe you don't know what your desires are yet. Either way, in **Beyond Your Wildest Dreams**, I am going to come alongside you and help you discover how to access, activate and achieve the your heart's desires. Let's not wait another moment before starting to improve your world!

There are lots of gift classes, think-and-get-rich programs and principles for living your dreams. But this book is unlike anything you have ever seen before because it is based on one simple truth—**the heart is the center from which all dreams flow**. The wise man, Solomon said, *"Above all else, guard your heart, for out of it flow the issues of life."* (Proverbs 4:23) The Hebrew word for "issues" is "source". The source of all the experiences of your life begins with your heart. The secret to having your dreams come true has been in front of us all along. It is a heart transformed by love which then sees and experiences life Beyond Your Wildest Dreams.

Lots of teaching is aimed at intellectual ideas which are good to shift our thinking, but then we wonder why it doesn't "stick". It is because information doesn't change anyone. Only heart transformation can do that. The ones who cooperate in the transformation of their own heart will easily change their experiences, and begin living and loving the life of their dreams.

We were all born with the same equipment, a spiritual heart, but the one who learns to steward it will get its joy and reward. Though this book is based on ancient spiritual and practical truths from the Bible, anyone of any religion, or no religion at all, can see it work for them. I believe God is a person and knowable but please don't get offended or distracted by that. Who I call God, you may call Spirit, Source, or Universe, and as a fellow traveler I can say with assurance that these truths work for all! So feel free to chew up the meat, and spit out any bones.

Our dreams are not discovered or fulfilled by outside sources anyway. Instead, love from the heart is the secret to it all! Love is a power that discovers, empowers, and creates the fulfillment of those dreams. The heart's vision, beliefs, feelings and intentions are like filters which can limit the expression of our inner power. As we shift our heart's vision, beliefs, feelings and intentions back to love, it creates a convergence which practically guarantees your dreams coming true.

Miracle of Transformation

I believe in miracles of all shapes and sizes. I personally witnessed and participated in many such as when three of us stood in a tiny hut in a little village in India and prayed for a bed-ridden woman who was unable to walk for ten years.

Suddenly she stood up and walked, to the surprise of everyone in her house. Several were watching through the windows and apparently when they saw this, they ran and shared it through the village, which began to line the street requesting prayers for their miracle too.

One time I prayed earnestly for a man who was blind. I would lay my hands over his eyes even as I prayed for others, then periodically check to see if there was any change. At some point among the large crowd of people I couldn't find him anymore. I asked the next day if our host knew the man, and he said, "Oh yes! He was born blind, but yesterday he began to see for the very first time!"

For the sake of transparency, I should tell you that many I've ministered to did not get a miracle. I share these with you because I want you to know that I know firsthand both extraordinary miracles and the difficulties of trying to figure out why something didn't happen for others. I never ever blame the receiver nor carry guilt when it didn't happen. I just chose to love and learn along the way.

Not all miracles are healings. While I was a broke college student, my wife wrote out our grocery list and hung it on the refrigerator. So we prayed, and the next day a fellow student was standing at our front door with bags of groceries. He was never in our home, nor ever saw the list, and was totally unaware of our need but what was on the list was in the bag!

I am so humbled and honored to be a small part of those stories. The same principles that caused my desires to come true, work for other areas of life as well. In each of those cases above, there was a change in me before there was a change outside of me.

What I've discovered is that the greatest miracle of all is my life transformed by, and into love. I use the word *transformed* intentionally because transformation is like a seed becoming a tree. All the DNA of a fully grown tree was in the seed to begin with, yet over time, it goes through stages of growth and maturity. It doesn't become another kind of tree. It matures out of its internal life and programing.

You are a good tree. The transformation of your life will not be found outside of yourself, in a change of lifestyle, nor perfect circumstances. It is found *in* you. It is found in the love that you receive and the love that you give, and when it comes to our dreams they can only be sustained by love.

The fact that you ordered this book is a sign, an indicator that you are about to hit a growth spurt. I love the saying, *"When the student is ready, the teacher will appear."* Somewhere in your heart, a belief that "there is more" drew you into this book. I believe that the truths that you discover here are going to change your life so thoroughly that you'll find yourself living an extraordinary life.

I discovered in my own life that there were latent dreams ready to emerge. You will discover them within you as well. There is a life to be lived that is so much more satisfying than what you are currently experiencing. I can't create it for you, but I can show you how to find your niche in life. It's not that hard because it's already within you. The secret is love. It is love that is attempting to draw it out, and your love for that dream that will bring it to you.

The Power of Love

Love is the *strength* that holds everything together.

Love is the *power* that set the stars in place.

Love binds relationships together.

Love heals the broken-hearted and binds up their wounds.

Love is the *source* of all that is good.

Love sets the adventurer on course.

Love changes the way we see ourselves and how we see the world.

Love is attractive.

Love that is sown returns a harvest of love.

Love that is given becomes a magnet drawing people into your life.

Love is a gift. Received from God it stabilizes and changes everything about your life—your goals expand, your limitations are removed, and your purpose changes. It is not so much about being commanded to love as it is being CREATED to love!

Love is not one among many attributes of God. It is the definition of His nature. God is love. His love is holy. His love is the truth of who He is to you. His love infuses all with His power.

Love is the life energy that motivates God himself. God is love. It is his eternal value, affection, and joy over all his creation!

Love is the most powerful thing in the universe.

In the Christian Bible the apostle James calls it the Law of Love! It is not the Law in the sense of an unyielding expectation *from* God, but because everything that exists was created from love, then the way of the universe in every dimension is love. To violate love is to tear the fabric of reality. The law of love is written into everything, and once you see it, you will see it everywhere. LOVE brings your desires to LIFE.

Love says it is okay for you to pursue your dreams. Want to climb Mt. Everest? Your love for climbing and God's love for you says, *go for it.* Want to fill a political office? Your love to serve and God's love for you says, *run!* Dreaming of a month-long vacation in the Caribbean? Your love for the sun, the sand, and blue waters along with God's love for you says, *you can have it.* Does your heart want children to hold as your own? Your love for children and God's love for you says *I will make a way!* Want to serve the poor in Haiti or the slums of India? Do you have a dream business or job in mind? It is possible. Nothing is impossible to those who believe in the power of love.

The Inside Scoop on Miracles:

"Either everything is a miracle or nothing is a miracle." –Albert Einstein

Everything really is a miracle, if you understand the definition of "miracle." In this book, I am using the generic word for *miracles*, but when we talk about miracles and your heart's desires, we need some better definitions than we were taught.

For a long time I thought miracles were those radical blessings that happened to me, but were unexplainable. Was it a formula, or did God randomly chose to give them to people. Maybe it was as a result of how well I prayed. But over the years I've learned that miracles and mystery are not always synonymous and it is no less a miracle if we can explain it.

What if miracles are not random acts of God? What if we have a say so in the experience? By making God responsible for every miracle, then it means we are also tempted to blame him for the non-performance of it, or conversely we think we or others didn't have "enough" faith for God to give it. Neither option is worthwhile.

When I began soul searching to discover the next steps in my own life, I not only had to follow the whispers in my heart, I had to be willing to participate in my heart so that they would come to pass. You will need heart participation too.

Some people think that a miracle is when God operates counter to the laws of nature. Because we tend to believe this, we call miracles "SUPER-natural". One of the things that quantum physics taught the scientific community is that there are completely different laws on the quantum level than at the atomic level. So too, a miracle doesn't violate nature; it just operates through different laws within creation, probably at a quantum level.

That is good news because if there is a way to cooperate with (not control) basic laws, then we can influence the outcomes, and if there is a part we play, then they don't have to be the exception. This Law is love.

I also learned that miracles are not a substitute for action. So together, wise action and miracle power create a capacity to achieve our hearts desires.

So what is a miracle? This is very important for us to understand. A superficial use of the word "miracle" will undermine the very nature of a miracle! The Greek word in the New Testament is the word, **dunamis**: *"(miraculous) power, might, strength"*. But notice Thayer's Greek definition: *"inherent power, power residing in a thing by virtue of its nature, or which a person or thing exerts and puts forth"*. Did you know that power is *inherent* within you now? The miracle is IN YOU now! It is learning how to release our miracle power through our hearts that causes us to manifest our dreams.

Jesus told a parable about how a man went on a journey and left five talents of money to one, two to another and one to yet another. He gave each one money according to his dunamis-power-ability, the same word for miracle in Greek. He knew each had varying levels of capacity in using his dunamis-power and expected a return on his investment. The one with five used his capacity to invest it and gain five more. The man with two gained two more. The one with one talent of money limited his God-given dunamis-power through fear and was rebuked for hiding it instead (Mt. 25:13-15).

In the story he limited his dunamis-power because of what he believed about the master. So too, what we believe about God affects the flow of our power. Love is the opposite of fear. Love opens the channels of our hearts so that it flows freely, and when it does amazing things will begin to happen!

Don't rush past this definition. If it is within us now, then how that dunamis-power flows through our words, our thoughts, our actions, our relationships and our dreams affects everything. We use it to create, to multiply or manifest dreams. Or we can allow it to be shut down, and shift the blame to God or the world around us. Micro and mega miracles flow through us, not just to us. The secret is in the plain truth of living from the inside out.

The dunamis-miracle-power of love causes us to act in new ways, to take on new tasks, and to increase our capacity for action. It empowers us to make real lasting changes, and to invest in projects we previously would be afraid of trying.

It also is a spiritual force flowing through us, that attracts our hearts desires into our lives and changes the environment around us. Some will call it favor. Others say that love is our highest vibration which attracts like experiences to like ideas. Whatever you call it, it is real and shapes our lives in ways that we are just barely starting to glimpse.

Beyond Your Wildest Dreams is not a new idea. It is an ancient enduring truth: *"Now to him who is able to do immeasurably **more** than all we **ask** or **imagine**, according to his **power** that is at work **within us**..."* (Ephesians 3:20, NIV). There is a miracle in you! Paul says it is the miracle-*dunamis*-power of love! The primary purpose was so that they would know God, but the outflow of that was to be into the human family and daily life. He is applying a general principle to the specific relationship. The general principle is that our God-given *dunamis*-power to know and flow in love, sets in motion more than we can ask or imagine!

Primary and Secondary Causes

There are two ditches we can fall into. One is to see the heart's power as nothing more than a natural technique for getting what we want, outside of a relationship with this very personal God. The other is to fall into the error of religion which attempts to manipulate God through rituals. Neither of these result in a satisfied life.

So it is important to remember at the outset that there are two causes of miracles. First, I personally believe that God is the ultimate source of every miracle, small and great by His power.

Second, when you notice the life and example of Jesus Christ, you will notice that He *never* asked the Father to heal anyone. Jesus had the authority from the Father to heal the sick, raise the dead, cleanse the lepers, calm storms, and multiply fish and loaves.

This is vital to understand because many times we are asking God to do something with our lives that He gave us the tools and the right to do ourselves. Yes, His loving presence is the primary source, but He has delegated authority over that creation to us. God is the primary cause, the original source, the prime mover, the life in all things. But you and I, and our choices to live in harmony with our design, possess an untapped exponential potential.

Chameleons are born with the ability to send a message from their brain to the cells of their skin, which mix colors and seemingly repaint themselves to communicate or blend into their environment. They have no ear openings, yet can detect sound frequencies. While they didn't create these powers within themselves, they do use it for their benefit. So too, your heart has great power, which didn't originate with you but is to be used for good as well.

Do you know what I am learning to use my heart to do? I love loving! I love teaching about love. I love coaching others to discover and reach their dream goals. I began to live from these truths, and I've watched doors open, opportunities unfold and life shift. That is why you have this book right now... it is part of my dream. Get ready to discover how to love your dreams into reality, too!

What to Expect

In this book, you are going to learn how to ACCESS the dreams in your heart, ACTIVATE them through your heart, and ACHIEVE them with your heart. The Law of love written on your heart is the secret to the life of which you have dreamed. As *your heart changes*, so will the world around you! I am continually challenged to mature in each of those areas simultaneously as my dreams get bigger and bigger.

There are 4 main parts of **Beyond Your Wildest Dreams: Access, Activate, and Achieve Your Heart's Desires:**

Part 1- THE SECRET TO FULFILLING YOUR DREAMS: You are Love's Mission
Part 2- WHO AM I? Transformed By Love
Part 3- UNCOVERING YOUR DREAM: Destiny Discovery
Part 4- STEP INTO YOUR FUTURE NOW: Manifesting the Miracle

Each section builds on the previous one. So I suggest that you make incremental steps allowing each one to saturate your heart until it becomes "real" to you, and then move on to the next section. Absorb them. Meditate on them. Become the truth.

Or you may also want to read all the way through, then come back and begin digging down. If you want personalized professional coaching, contact us and we will help you get through any places were you are hung up.

Please note that this book is not a formula, but it is practical. It is filled with wisdom about your heart, and once you become aware of how powerful your heart is, you will learn to experience your heart's desires!

In order to help you to fully embody the truth of each chapter, I created exercises at the end of each one that are designed to make your heart more aware of it. ***Don't skip the exercises.*** Information doesn't change anyone. It simply makes us feel like we know more. True knowledge and understanding is an experience of the heart. The exercises are the life of this book!

Here is an important truth: *Nothing in the book will help you in any way, whatsoever... unless you put it into practice!* Each of these exercises is designed to build on the previous one, so embrace the process. DO NOT SKIP THE EXERCISES!

THE EFFECTIVENESS OF THIS BOOK IS IN THE EXERCISES!

In each chapter you will also discover a *Heart Truth* that is key to knowing, experiencing, manifesting and receiving the love that will make your dreams come true! Scientific research is only now discovering what students of Scripture and intuitive leaders have known for centuries.

Heart Truth 1—It Is a Change of Heart That Changes Things.

It isn't a change of thoughts that change things; it is a change of heart. Our primary "effort" is allowing changes in our heart from which everything flows!

The Institute of Heart Math Research Center has dedicated itself to discovering the mysteries of the heart. What they have discovered is amazing. For instance, here are some truths they found:

- ☐ The heart gives off a magnetic field of energy 5,000 times stronger than the thoughts in our brains. It can be measured several feet away from our bodies and it changes depending on our emotions.
- ☐ Negative emotions of the heart can create chaos in the nervous system of the body.
- ☐ The heart contains memory neurons for both short and long term memory. In other words, as other science has demonstrated, our memories are not held primarily in the brain, but in every cell in our body, but in particular in the heart.
- ☐ Positive emotions that begin in the heart have the capacity to send signals to the brain that aid in creativity.
- ☐ Did you know that the heart is formed in the child in the womb and starts beating *before* the brain develops?
- ☐ The heart sends more information to the brain than the brain does to the heart. (https://www.heartmath.org/about-us/videos/mysteries-of-the-heart/)

Paul, the apostle, tells us that it's always ***the natural first, and then the spiritual***. The heart works from the same principle (1 Cor. 15:46). The natural heart is amazing and its incredible importance teaches us about the value of our spiritual heart.

According to Scripture the heart is the place from which we believe, therefore, how we relate to God through our hearts is the most important part of knowing Him and affects our whole life. As the ancient proverb tells us, ***"As a man thinks in his heart, so is he."***

For too long our Western brain-focused logic culture has tried to change people through every method other than the one that works: heart change. Many don't realize how easy our dreams come true once they learn to harness the power of love through the heart. I am so excited for you to discover it!

This verse has helped me focus the flow of my life: ***"the purpose of our instruction is love, from a pure heart, a pure conscience, and a sincere faith"*** (1 Tim. 1:5). Everything that you will discover is nothing more than learning how to live *and* love your dream into reality. So thank you for being a part of this unique book that is destined to give you the tools to change your inner and outer life.

PART 1

THE SECRET TO FULFILLING YOUR DREAMS:
You are Love's Mission

Authentic You: The Mission of Love

"Don't be born an original and die a copy" –John Mason

Let's face it. You are absolutely amazing. Stunning! You are a fascinating expression of the handiwork of God. Didn't know that? Don't quite believe it? Hang on, because you are now entering into a great adventure Beyond Your Wildest Dreams.

Your most important mission is not in discovering a cure for cancer, or discovering another galaxy, or becoming a millionaire. Those things can certainly happen. In fact, when you discover the real *you*, those type things could happen much easier than you know. I want you to be a millionaire. I want you to discover a cure that changes the world. It's just that the real mission of your life is first and foremost, *you*. That's right. In order to fulfill your dreams, you need to begin with **you**.

Others have told you that you must put God first, others second, and yourself last. Especially if you are a mom, right? But the model for my life is how Jesus put His identity as a son first in relationship with His Father, and only then, and only out of that place was He ready to serve others and fulfill His purpose. Sonship first, labor as the expression. He knew who He was and where He was going. Do you? Well, you will soon enough.

The inner purpose of your life and a major secret to living Beyond Your Wildest Dreams is to be "you", as loved by God. Read that sentence again please. God is on a love mission, and it is for you to be you!

When God created Adam and Eve He said that they were created in His image. Yet the man is different than the woman. The man and the woman each display slightly unique aspects of the image of God. Differences aren't denials of the image of God. One is not more "right" than the other. So also it is in discovering and living from the most authentic version of *you* as you begin to display your true colors. As you step into authenticity, you begin to discover your outward purposes.

The greatest changes that took place in my life were when I stopped trying to be someone else in any way. I grew up with a divorced mother who worked two jobs, so I didn't have my parent's presence to teach me about how life works. They weren't there for me to ask important life questions. So subconsciously I suppose I watched others to determine what was the "right" way to be and live, instead of trusting my authentic self. Unfortunately, the problem is that everyone has their own version, and most aren't living through authenticity either.

So learning to really embrace the authenticity of my own life was incredibly life-giving. Nothing is more empowering than the freedom to be who you choose to be regardless of what others think or demand.

So welcome to the awakening. For a long time maybe you have lived someone else's version of you. Your mission is to be you, discover your authenticity and then live from it.

Manufacturers often tell us to only use their genuine parts. Cheap aftermarket substitutes tend to cause the machine to not function at its optimum level. The same is true for you. Authenticity is when you are in sync with the real you!

I know this resonates with you because every person is born with a design that is so perfect that the only way to miss it is to cover it up with fear. Sometimes our greatest fear is not an end of the world scenario, but the fear of feeling alive in our own skin. Or it is the fear that who we are and what we have is defective or destined to rejection. *But there is no fear in love.* When you accept that you are perfectly loved it will begin to drive out fear.

So go ahead and embrace the unconditional, all inclusive love that God has for you and the purposes that are within you. You aren't called to be civil rights leader, Dr. Martin Luther King, nor William Wilberforce who fought for the abolition of the slave trade, or anybody else for that matter. We can only be inspired by them to bravely pursue our own purposes. Your calling is to be *you*. Don't be a poor copy of someone else. Be alive and accept the value of who you are as a fully loved human being!

I read the top ten regrets of the elderly from a well-known study in Australia by a woman named Bronnie Ware. Here is what she said their end of life regrets were:

1. I never pursued my dreams and aspirations.
2. I worked too much and never made time for my family.
3. I should have made more time for my friends.
4. I should have said 'I love you' a lot more.
5. I should have spoken my mind instead of holding back and resenting things.
6. I should have been the bigger person and resolved my problems.
7. I wish I had children.
8. I should have saved more money for my retirement.
9. Not having the courage to live truthfully.
10. Happiness is a choice; I wish I'd known that earlier. –

(See more at: http://www.bronnieware.com/blog/regrets-of-the-dying)

Did you notice what was number one? **The main regret of those at the end of their lives was that they never pursued their dreams or aspirations to a satisfying degree.** That is not a regret that I want. Nor do I believe that it is yours either. That is why you are here. You are here because you believe there is something more to life. There is an inner longing for the *real you* to come out.

I also believe that it's true of dreams and destinies within us. They never go away. They are right under the surface, trying to break through like seeds breaking through the soil of our hearts. Many of those dreams speak a language that is different than we are accustomed to interpreting, so they remain nebulous and ethereal. But they are there because you are there.

The prophet Samuel came to the soon-to-be King Saul saying, *"I am the seer. Go up before me to the high place, for you shall eat with me today; and tomorrow I will let you go and will tell you all that is in your heart"* (1 Sam. 9:19, AMPC).

The prophet-seer Samuel said that everything that was in Saul's future was already in his heart. Did you see that? Saul didn't know what was there, and the only reason Samuel did is because he was gifted to see it. Prophetic people aren't giving you something incongruous with what is already in your heart. So if you want to find your destiny, you will find it *within* yourself!

I find when I coach others I can often help them discover their genuine selfs, but I don't ever create it. It was already there.

Dreams are not found from an outside source telling us to

conform to their vision. They are not found in an organization shouting to our fears. They are not found in parents who want *our* best but want us to fulfill *their* unfulfilled dreams. The life of fulfillment is found in the beauty of uncovering and living from the real you, the authentic you. The world needs you, no matter what others might have said.

So let's address this right at the beginning: in order for authenticity to be activated in your life, you must embrace one powerful principle, the **Law of Love**. This love is not reserved for only loving God. God loves *you*. You were created out of love.

Jesus said we are to love our neighbors. We also learn that we are to love even our enemies. How then can you disqualify *yourself*? You are your closest neighbor. If God loves you, then to take an opinion other than His about you is to bring yourself into disharmony with all that you are. Authenticity means starting by valuing yourself as *loved*. So climb on board and let's take the journey together.

Heart Truth 2—The Heart Is Designed to Function in the Present Tense.

Ever felt limited or distracted by the *"cares of this world"*? By seeing life as a "distraction" we miss that all of life is sacred, from washing dishes, to selling furniture, to praying with fervor, to making love with your spouse. ***Whatsoever things you do, do all to the glory of God.***

The root of the word ***"cares"*** means to **"divide"**. In other words, the cares of this life are any time we find ourselves divided and pulled into either the past or the future. The heart was not created to live in anywhere other than the ***now***. Even hope regarding the future is just confidence right *now* that good is coming our way.

So this simple exercise is to help you come out of distraction into the present. As they say, that is why it is called "the presence" of God. That is why we should quit being driven to pray for God to come, to show up, to visit us or other silly language. The truth is that He is here right *now*. He is **I AM**. He is Emmanuel, God with us!

You cannot find the real "you" in the past nor in the future. You are here now. If your past continues to define your future, you will never be able to escape it. Only discovering who God says you are NOW and embracing His definition, will you truly be able to disconnect from the imaginary you of the past.

The skill of living in the now is used in every field of life. In sales or counseling when the client is on an emotional roller coaster, living in the now is staying present with them, instead of reacting to their problems or objections. In marriage, it is being fully available instead of our minds being somewhere else while we feign attention. It keeps us from being distracted by worry and makes us fully engaged in the test we are taking. It makes worship something meaningful instead of our hearts being far from God. It is the place where we simply rest in a trust that calms the cacophony of thoughts vying for our attention.

The psalmist said, *"Be still and know that I am God."*

Though you can do this anywhere at any time, I suggest you find a place where you won't be interrupted. Have a pen and journal ready for an exercise.

Heart Truth 3—Your Heart Is the Conduit Between the Spirit and the Soul.

Our heart is influenced either from the inside-out (spirit), or the outside-in (soul). So we need to learn how to still and quiet so that the voice of the soul (emotions, random thoughts) can quiet and we can begin to draw from the spirit.

Don't misunderstand. This doesn't mean you have to go naval-gazing. You don't need to wear an orange robe and shave your head in order to enjoy the benefits of purposeful quieting. In fact, the more you know who *Christ* is, the more you will understand how amazing *you* are! Serenity belongs to everyone.

Let me encourage you to a practice so simple that it goes unnoticed by many because it doesn't appear "spiritual". It is breathing. One of the very first expressions of God to man was that He breathed into him and made him a living soul. Breathing is an extremely important aspect of our lives, as everyone held under the water by a mean older brother can testify!

Yes, I know you are doing that right now, but most of us breathe with the upper part of our lungs essentially mimicking the same rhythm and shallow breathing of anxiety. In other words we are sometimes making ourselves anxious simply by our breathing habits.

Doing these exercises along with deep belly-breathing will help pull you away from feelings of anxiety (divided time cares of this world) so that you can focus on what is most important. *Breath is to the body and soul what life is to the spirit.* You already have life in your spirit, so you can bring greater alignment in your soul by learning to breathe differently.

As an aside, I lost ten pounds as a byproduct of doing this. Just by breathing differently for about 45 minutes a day for one month it changed my metabolism. I ate the same but lost weight effortlessly. I'm not promising you a ten-pound weight loss, but it can happen. Stress releases cortisol which increases appetite. More oxygen means your body will burn more calories. That is how powerful a simple change in breathing can affect your body. So imagine what can also happen in your soul after one month!

The NOW Exercise
Purpose: To reconnect our hearts to the present moment.

We are in such a habit of not being authentic, that we are in need of practicing ways to help us find that place. Please be very strategic in rediscovering the real you. When our heart truths are combined with practical habits and exercises, they begin to become second nature to us. That is exactly what we need so that we don't sabotage ourselves on the journey.

The Breath Prayer and Noticing Exercise

By practicing the Breathe Prayer or the Noticing Exercise, you are getting your heart into the present moment where it can more easily be changed, noticed, and listened to. Many times we "guarded our heart" in error and we don't know how to change out the guard that has been on duty for a long time. Getting the heart into the present makes your heart more impressionable for what you want to deposit, because it is how you begin to change the "guard" beliefs that stand watch there.

In fact, this is nothing new. Breath and prayer were connected as a spiritual discipline known as "Breath prayer", or "the Jesus Prayer" or "Prayer of the Heart" dating back to at least the sixth century. Historically, it is has been honored within the more contemplative streams like the Eastern Church.

Early believers would repeat simple phrases from Scripture to the rhythm of their breath, such as" Lord Jesus, have mercy."

Christian mystic, Thomas Merton, suggests this method. Even well-known writer, Richard Foster, said that *Breath Prayer* was one of the fundamental expressions of unceasing prayer. So the connection between the natural rhythms of breathing and the spiritual life is an ancient Christian practice.

For a way to do this exercise in the future, you could use the Hebrew name for God, Yahweh. The name means "I am that I am". Breathe in saying "Yah" and out saying "weh". Then "I am"… "that I am". Focus on the words as you breathe them in and out. Feel their meaning. By focusing on the now, and setting yourself in the context of His love and presence, you will get the results described below. You can combine the awareness exercise and the breath prayer if you like. Continue until your heart feels at rest and in peace.

Once you get a feel for the exercise below, you can use the breath prayer without the "noticing" exercise I am about to teach you.

When we pay attention to what is going on in the now, and notice without judging everything, we will find ourselves in the present moment. The present is where God lives. Start by taking a moment and breathing in, and imagine you are breathing in God's love for you, and as you breathe out imagine love coming back out of you into the world around you. Maybe see love as a color and notice it coming in and then back out again.

So close your eyes, put your hand over your heart. Breathe in through your nose and out through your mouth in slow natural rhythms again. Simply notice things. The key is to not judge them as good or bad. Don't figure out a plan to change them. Simply notice. That is all you are going to do... observe without commentary on meaning, or judging it as a problem... just notice.

Notice the way the air feels coming into your body and going back out again. With each breath pay attention to how it makes your body feel. Now notice the clothes that you are wearing. How do they feel on your body? Where do they move as you breathe in and out? What about your skin? Do you feel the temperature in the room? Notice the temperature of the air on your skin. What do you hear? Simply discern the variety of sounds all around you.

All these things are happening in the now. This is where you are. This is where God dwells. He is **I Am**. As you sit in His presence He is with you. He is for you. He loves you. Take a moment and thank Him for His love. Thank Him for your unique design and ask Him to begin helping you to enjoy being you.

(You can also immerse yourself in nature somewhere, which has the same calming effect.)

Once you are done ask yourself: "how did I feel" or "what did I sense?" Usually when I first introduce someone to this exercise the most common response is peace. Journal your results.

Be Amazed At Yourself: You Glow in the Dark!

"But I don't want to go among mad people," Alice remarked.
"Oh, you can't help that," said the Cat: "we're all mad here. I'm
mad. You're mad."
"How do you know I'm mad?" said Alice.
"You must be," said the Cat, "or you wouldn't have come here."
—Lewis Carroll, *Alice in Wonderland*

"You must be crazy!" That is a matter of perspective isn't it? But here you are. You've come to this book for a reason and the life that is coming to you might make others think that you bumped your head and went mad. Yet when you discover the wonderland of love inside of you, what they call crazy, will be your norm… and you'll be thankful for it. You will begin living your dream while awake and you'll join all those crazy "mad" people who are living their dreams, too!

At one point in my life I embraced a form of religious legalism that taught me the belief that there was something inherently wrong with me, and that subtle shame began to creep into everything I did, limiting my dreams. Then I found a truth I want to share with you. I discovered this nugget in 2 Timothy 1:9, ***"who has saved us and called us with a holy calling, not according to our works, but according to His own purpose and grace which was given to us in Christ Jesus before time began"*** (KJV).

Did you know that God imagined us in grace *before* we ever fell into any self-destructive behavior or lost our way to our dreams? God purposed to deliver us by grace before we ever got twisted up in life. Jesus said your Father knows your needs before you even ask Him. He pre-planned answers before you thought of the problem. He has always been proactive!

That verse also means he had a relationship toward you in his heart before creation. He was relating to us through love as he formed you in your mother's womb. The day you were *birthed* the Father and the angels celebrated, the Son put His hands on your little baby head and spoke a blessing over you. He had affection for you while you were sowing wild oats, patiently waiting for you to come to your senses. He was with you all the times that you imagined you were utterly alone. It means that when you made bad decisions, *He was more concerned about you seeing the answer instead of seeing the problem.*

The good news is not about you creating a relationship with God in order to satisfy Him, but about announcing that God has been working in your life through grace since before creation. On His side of the equation, He declares through the Apostle Paul, **"God was in Christ reconciling the world to Himself, NOT counting men's sins against them."** Hearing that announcement wakes up our hearts and changes us.

Is that the end of the story though? Paul prayed for the Ephesians to have *the Spirit of Revelation in the knowledge of God... that the eyes of their <u>heart</u> would be enlightened and that they would know what is the hope of his calling and...* (NOTICE THIS)—what are *the riches of the glory of His inheritance <u>IN</u> the saints*! The word "riches" means "more than enough"! The inheritance of Jesus from the Father, is shared with you! It is already in you. It is glorious life!

So God pre-ordained more than enough glorious love, light, and life in you to fulfill every dream of your heart!

I remember a pastor that once forbid his members to clap their hands to show appreciation for the gifting of a person after they finished singing because *"God will not share His glory with another."* Yet, that passage from Isaiah is speaking of wood and stone idols that could not give life. He was saying they can't adequately represent him. Isaiah 42:8 says, *"I am the LORD, that is My name; and My glory I will not give to another, nor My praise to carved images"* (NAS).

God, on the other hand, has shared His glory with *you*. He placed His image within you. He joined His glory to the real you. Even more, Jesus made a profound statement in John 17:22, *"I have given them the glory that you gave Me, that they may be one as We are one"* (NIV).

You are one with God. Did you know that? Paul said in 1 Corinthians 6:17 that your spirit and His Spirit have become one; *you have become one with the Lord.* God joined His glory to your spirit! *You are way more amazing than you ever imagined.* You are no accident. You are not the product of a random sexual encounter between two people, nor an evolutionary biological product. YOU are a glorious, luminescent, beautiful being filled with power, strength, purpose and divine life. You are glorious. If you were to turn on a spiritual black light, you would be glowing in the dark! For too long you've defined yourself from the outside-in when all that God does is from the inside-out.

Paul said in Galatians 1:16, *"It pleased the Lord to reveal Christ IN me."* Not just *to* me, but *within* me! You are beyond words! You are marked with divinity. The superlatives are insufficient to describe the living image of God inside of you! When God looks at you, he sees himself. It's called the image and likeness of God in you!

If you peel back the false or inadequate definitions you can see the truth. Take away all the trophies, the skills, the accolades, the words meant to demean. Take away all the labels of mother, father, sister, brother… take away the male and female distinctions… remove your job title or lack of one, remove ethnicity and nationality… underneath it all, who are you, really?

You are a being joined to God in your spirit, filled with glorious life, light, love, wisdom and power. You are more than a physical body. If you lose a limb, would you cease being you? No, because your body isn't the definition of the essence of you. The real you is mind-blowing!

Pay close attention to what Jesus said one day. *"Let YOUR light so shine before men that they may see your good works and glorify your Father in heaven."* He said YOUR light. He isn't ashamed of your light, your spark, your uniqueness. He is thrilled by it because He put it there. He is not ashamed to call us family. You are a glorious being joined to the Creator of all things. You are luminescent in His sight. As YOU shine through your life and actions, it will, by default, glorify your Father in heaven. As people often hear me say, *the only thing that is wrong with you is that you think that there's something wrong with you.*

"God is light and in Him is no darkness at all." One of the characteristics of light is that its effusion is always outward. God is always shining; it is the nature of His being. You too are filled with light, truth, good and grace intended to shine out through your life in your smile, your words, your ideas, plans, personality, creativity and every conceivable way. You are never more authentic than when you are in that unhindered state of not being self-conscious, but rather just lost in the flow of "being"

you to others.

The limits of our lives are the ones we placed there or embraced there. The limits are based on who we see in the mirror. Our beliefs about ourselves and how God relates to us are the locks and lids on our lives. They are steel plates trying to shut out the light of truth and concrete side-walks blocking the nourishment of the rain from a small seed buried underground. But like Jesus' resurrection, the good things in us are rising up.

Are you in danger of pride by thinking well of yourself? Not at all. Pride says, ***"I will ascend to the heavens, I will sit on the mount with God, I will..."*** But what others tried to do by effort, God has given you by grace. You are seated with Christ in the heavenly places, and you did nothing to get there. It simply is. It is now. It is true.

So too, the simple acknowledgment that grace gave you this life, is humility. Pride is our constant striving to become something that we already are. Otherwise, we run the risk of making conservative decisions about who we are and then hide in order to be accepted. We fear rocking the boat or expressing our true nature. I tend to agree with comedian, Jim Carrey's commencement speech in which he said, "The need for acceptance can actually make you invisible. Risk being seen in all your glory."

When I hold back, shrink down and minimize my value, I am obscuring the light of love that impacts the world. The world is robbed of you and the flavor that was needed for our generation. Be it large or small, we were born to manifest the powerful light of love within us.

You might be thinking, *"If I live according to who I think I am,*

I might just shoot somebody!" Well, when you know your inner essence is made out of love, then you will start valuing the uniqueness of others, and seeing about them what they can't see in themselves. We cannot give away what we don't think we possess.

THE KINGDOM OF GOD IS LIKE A MAN WHO FOUND TREASURE HIDDEN IN A FIELD AND FOR THE JOY OVER IT GOES AND SELLS ALL THAT HE HAS SO THAT HE CAN HAVE THAT TREASURE.
JESUS IS THE MAN. **YOU** ARE THE TREASURE!

Paul made this extraordinary statement in Philemon 1:6, *"That the communication of thy faith may become effectual by the acknowledgment of every good thing which is in you in Christ Jesus"* (KJV). That verse gets translated so many different ways, but the word "communication" is the word for sharing. It means that as your heart shares God's heart, and you acknowledge all the good things that are in you because of what he put there, it will cause your beliefs to become effective!

This is a Beyond Your Wildest Dreams key! Miracles come from *dunamis*-power within! So value what is within you!

Be amazed at yourself! You glow in the dark!

Remember Alice in Wonderland being concerned about being "mad"? What is maddening is living a dualistic belief in which you are told you are evil at heart… yet you are expected to live righteously. Then threatened with excommunication and hell if you don't do what you were just told you were incapable of doing. That kind of foolishness and psychological damage creates a fatalistic approach to your life. It drains away any hope because it is practically impossible to live beyond your own view of yourself. Learn to let go of the false view of yourself by consciously embracing the truth.

Gump Glory

God is about the business of ***revealing the glory that is within us*** (Romans 8:18). Did you ever think about that? He has purposed to draw that glory out from within you, so who are you to hide the light that is called *you*?

Ralph Waldo Emerson said, "What lies before you and what lies behind you are tiny matters compared to what lies within you."

The essence of who you are is a spirit of love. You are a new creation. You might have habits of thought inconsistent with the new you. You could possess feelings from your past. But if you define yourself according to your past, you are doomed to not only keep repeating it, but you will never fully access the dream in your heart. No one wants to reach into their heart if they think it is filled with darkness.

Instead, it is love that put dreams there. That's why you can't find it outside yourself. You can hear encouragement from others. You might discover by experience that you have a love for painting, for instance, that you didn't know was there. I can show you steps to re-discovering YOU. But the good news is that it is already there. YOU are the dream of God's heart and your uniqueness isn't in trying to be like others, but by being your divine self!

This is where it begins... falling in love with *you*. Valuing *you*! Your destiny begins in no other place than agreeing with the grace given to you in your own being before time began! That means that all the purposes for your life are coded into your inner spirit already. You aren't God, but you are a divine being with a spirit coded with a DNA just like your physical DNA. There are things you are designed to do that will only happen if you are authentically you. Forrest Gump lived life to the fullest and impacted the world by being Gump!

When I started to realize this, I found that my dream was tied to helping others discover this for themselves. Very few things delight me as much as helping people see the treasure within them. So finding the value in myself became the catalyst for my own dream! I constantly search for ways to help people see the truth of themselves. I look at others and wish I could give them a spiritual MRI and watch them stare in wonder at themselves.

The God-In-Me Exercise
Purpose: To develop a habit of noticing your amazing awesomeness

Prayer: "Father, thank you for your glory that you share with me. I want to acknowledge every good thing in me. Reveal that glorious life, light and life to me, in me and through me."

Now write down every good thing that is in you because of this truth. Make a list. Allow yourself to write until you exhaust everything you can imagine as true about you. If you don't know what those things are, ask a trusted friend or your spouse to write down a list of everything that they like about you. Humility isn't self-degradation. It is the honest view of ourselves based on what God has done for us. This is not the time for judging those things; just write them, whatever comes up out of your heart.

Thank you that I am (write them in the space below)…

Releasing Your Inner Awesome: The Power of Beliefs

"Situations do not change us, rather it is the meaning we assign to them and the beliefs that result."

You have an incredible power. It is the power of personal choice. God, Himself, will not violate your will, nor force you to do anything. After looking at the limitations of my own life and trying many methods of changing, I came back to this simple truth: the greatest use of my *dunamis*-power of love is to choose to believe the truth about the real me. Remember, this is not the *you* that your ex-spouse has tried to tell you. It's not the "you" defined by aloneness, powerlessness, hopelessness and pain. That is not the real you. The real you is awesome, fearfully and wonderfully made. The real you has power and it is the power to *believe*. Or as Paul said, *"love believes all things"* which some suggest means "believes the best of others" but at its core love "believes".

The Life that Belief Built

This may come as a shock to you, but your world is largely made up of what your beliefs have built. We think that we are limited by our environment, our family up-bringing, our social status, our bank account or our education. Those are not limitations. We sometimes think that maybe God is the One holding us back waiting for us to qualify for something good when you are *already qualified* (Colossians 1:12). Jesus made it very clear, **"nothing is impossible with God"** and **"all things are possible to him that believes!"**

Don't confuse what I am teaching as blame for not having "enough" faith. This is not about a faith-based measuring stick to get God to "move". This is about how we live and experience life through our belief systems.

Nor am I talking about the silliness that we were taught to lie to ourselves saying, "I'm not sick" while coughing and hacking at the doctors office. Or even when we avoid medical care altogether thinking that it is faith. It isn't.

Instead, think about the life that our beliefs build. Why do you drive the ragged car that you drive? Now think of all the beliefs that are involved which could be limiting you. Is it literally the only car in the world that you could afford? Or did you buy it on impulse because you believed someone else was going to get it before you? Did you believe that you couldn't get a slightly better income or that this is the kind of car that fits your view of yourself as a slightly poor college student? You might say that it's because it was the only one you could afford. Or you might say it was a gift and it would hurt the feelings of the one who gave it to you if you got another one. There are many beliefs that went into you getting that car.

This goes for every thing that is going on in your life. The color of the walls of your house, the kind of job you have, the friends that you attract, or the amount of money that you make. In reality, they are all coming from our own personal beliefs that create the environment that we live in. It is actually very empowering to discover that most of our life is the direct result of our own choices arising out of our own beliefs.

Let's consider finances. Maybe you grew up in a poor family and you heard words like *"rich people are thieves"* (which isn't a universal truth) or *"the Bible says money is the root of all evil"* (which it doesn't). Let's say that you also have a view of yourself that says you aren't worth very much. What happens when someone offers you a better job making amazing money for your gifts and skills? In your heart, probably without realizing it, you may be driven to turn the job down. Or if you also believe you really *need* the money and take the job, eventually you would sabotage yourself because you will never *feel* as if you deserve it.

As Albert Einstein said, *"We cannot solve our problems with the same thinking we used when we created them."* Or we could say, *"We cannot solve our problems with the same beliefs we used to create them."*

Consider the woman who is living in an abusive relationship. Her husband beats her and her children, and one day he may very well kill her. She hates the abuse, but she can't imagine changing it. She can't see anything beyond what is her normal, and she believes his propaganda that if she leaves, he will kill her. She may even have beliefs pounded into her by a hyper-religious church that says God will hate her if she ever gets a divorce.

Most of us looking on the outside can't fathom why she would stay in that situation, but her life is built on one thing...her own beliefs. All this is happening while she is praying for God to do something for her that she isn't willing to do for herself. She prays for God to change the situation while He is the One trying to change her beliefs and get her to act out of those beliefs. Do you see why our beliefs are so powerful? We live in a magical fairyland mentality waiting on God to change something when it is our beliefs he is trying to change!

So you see, our entire world of experiences is made up of the limitations or the expansion of our own beliefs. We don't actually live according to our desires. We live according to the expectation that our beliefs create. That means your dream can only come true by changing what you believe. *If you build it, your dream will come!* If you allow God to change your opinion about Him and about yourself, you will find amazing things happening in your life!

So who is in control of your life? It's not what some other person did to you; don't give them the authority to permanently ruin your life. You get to set the course. Wayne Dyer once perceptively said, *"If you think other people are the cause of your problems, you're going to have to send the rest of the world to the psychiatrist for you to get better."* Ultimately our problem isn't what others do or say. Not even God will force you to believe. Instead He invites you to let Him awaken trust in your heart.

The Master Keys to Changing Beliefs:

Sometimes we say, "I know in my head that it's true, but I can't seem to get it from my head to my heart!" The best explanation I've heard is to imagine a giant iceberg…the tip of the iceberg is your conscious mind, but the huge part underneath the water—what I call the heart, and others might call the subconscious—is the part that actually controls our actions, our emotions, our beliefs and therefore, our destiny. Most programs focus on changing our thinking, which is the only the tip. In order to understand this, we need to think about the way that beliefs control our lives.

Heart Truth 4—The Heart's Beliefs Form an Authority System

Not all beliefs were created equal. There are some beliefs that we are open to change our opinion about with very little evidence and very little time. For instance, you may believe that you don't like broccoli and then the next minute after tasting it with warm melted cheese you completely change your belief. Of course, with broccoli that could never happen.

On the other hand, you may believe very strongly in something and no one can convince you otherwise. These are beliefs that we "know" are true and we say they are in our "heart of hearts." Yet they may not be true. The reason is that our hearts have established a hierarchy of beliefs that are connected and we live at their control.

Our hearts perceive some beliefs as having greater authority than others. As a result, we sometimes feel conflicted and a sense of violating our conscience because one belief says that I need money to pay my bills and enjoy life while a more powerful belief says that God teaches that money is the root of all evil. Until the more powerful, core-level belief is changed, all our actions will either feel like we are about to face negative consequences because we violated the big belief, or we will allow the wrong belief to continue to sabotage our lives and limit our dreams.

So while changing surface level beliefs does help temporarily, most of the time we are focused on changing those, when in actuality it is our innermost universal governing beliefs that are ruling our lives. That is why religious habits that focus on the outside never work. All of God's work is an inside job! So one of the most effective ways to live Beyond Your Wildest Dreams is to cooperate in changing what I call **Global Governing Beliefs**, so that it will, by virtue of that change, work its way out to all the other beliefs over time.

Alan Tutt, in his book *Choose to Believe: A Practical Guide to Living Your Dreams*, wrote about the belief hierarchy dividing it into four main categories: Universal Beliefs, World Beliefs, Self-Image Beliefs, and Surface Beliefs. Universal Beliefs form the core of our being.

The beliefs with the greatest authority are Universal (Global Governing Beliefs) about God (probably because of the truth found in Ecclesiastes that *God put eternity in our hearts.*) These are beliefs about God and his nature, character, personality, plans and his expectations of us. World Beliefs are about the world in general and particularly about how we see people. Self-Image beliefs are about ourselves in general and how we fit into the world. Surface Beliefs are about specific situations, events and things in life.

This is a very accurate way of understanding. I would only suggest instead of a top down hierarchy, think of it as concentric circles that move outward with lesser degrees of importance and authority. God beliefs form the core and greatest authority, even if it was a belief there is no God.

For example, if you believe that God is mostly angry, then that will affect your world beliefs and how you view people. We become like the god we trust, so we too will be angry with others. It will influence how you see yourself, since you will wonder what is wrong with you that you can't get it together and please God. Then it will affect surface level beliefs because you will interpret any bad thing that happens as a form of angry punishment from God for wrong-doing. The core belief affects all the other beliefs.

Let's say your dream is to make a difference in politics by providing an optimistic perspective and planning for future generations, but you have a subtle universal belief that says God is ending the world soon. That core belief will short circuit your own dreams without you realizing it.

Or maybe you believe God's love is conditional. So then you will see the world as needing to earn love. Your children will have to perform perfectly before getting any affection. No one will feel they can live up to your expectations and others never receive affirmation. Every God belief has implications.

Generally speaking, they are all linked together, like a pebble in a pond sending ripples outward to all other beliefs. So trying to change your view about people without changing your view about God results in internal conflict, and creates difficulty in trying to change that belief.

I remember hearing the phrase, "God is in a good mood", and the more I thought about it, the more I questioned. The more I questioned, the more I was pulled into a journey of deciding if I really believed it was true. As I dug deeper into the topic I started letting go of beliefs contrary to the goodness and love of God, and eventually it completely changed my world. I taught differently, saw life clearer, and became more courageous to share that truth because of how much I knew God loved me with his goodness. It eventually created major changes in the direction of my life, and I can't tell you how much joy came as a result of it!

What a liberating day when I had the courage to fully accept the Apostle Paul's words, *"Not that we lord it over your faith, but we are fellow workers with you for your joy..."* (2 Cor. 1:24, BSB). No one has the right to coerce another to believe something. If we are forced to believe something out of fear, then we are actually trusting fear. Instead we are looking for those truths that produce the fruit of faith, hope, love and joy in us, and when we find them, we get to incorporate them into our lives. There is only one overarching filter now for my life, and that is the all inclusive, unconditional love of God.

<u>Power Truth #1</u>: Being willing to change our beliefs about God at the Global Governing Beliefs level, will create a powerful ripple effect through our whole life.

Consider this for a moment. We all initially learn interpretations of God from our family, from a trusted source, a book. a pastor or teacher that we love. When our interpretation is challenged, it feels awkward and threatening because we value not just the teaching but the one who taught us. We associate the teacher with the message. As a result, we find it hard to believe something different. But is that how we discover and embrace truth?

People are also often afraid of what the truth will cost them. It might mean losing our status with a denomination, a spiritual group or losing friendships that are close. Isn't it possible that God may want to give you a new perspective, and if so, are you willing to allow Him? Isn't it possible that they too are being limited by the same beliefs? Some will resist how you are changing your beliefs, but many times it will spark courage for others after they see its effect in your life!

Churches, denominations and spiritual groups tend to be built around a system of beliefs, a list of what they consider fundamental truths. What happens if we are more loyal to a list of beliefs than we are to God himself? What happens if HE wants to change one of your beliefs about Him? If we are more loyal to the system, than to ourselves and our authentic heart, we have essentially locked ourselves into a life which will never change.

Here is a list of some beliefs on the **universal level**. Rate the strength of your belief from 1 to 10, with 1 being a very weak belief, to 10 meaning you strongly believe. In order for this to be effective you will need to ask yourself not what is the right answer, but in your heart, *what feels true*? This is especially true about universal level beliefs because in our hearts we may actually believe God is better than what we have been told, but we are afraid (a belief) that we can't be honest about it.

1. I believe that there is a God.
2. I believe that God is judging my behavior.
3. I believe that God is friendly and loves life.
4. I believe that God's love is all inclusive.
5. I believe that God's love is unconditional.
6. I believe that God forgave me before I asked.
7. I believe that God is harsh with me.
8. I believe that God fully accepts me as his child just as I am.
9. I believe God wants to teach me to fulfill my dreams.
10. I believe in miracles and that they can be common in my life.
11. I believe that God turns everything in my life around for good.
12. I believe that I am a spiritual being in a human body with a soul.
13. I believe that it's ok to want good things or better things in my life.
14. I believe that wealth, money and spirituality are compatible.

15. I believe that life is playful like a dog wagging its tail.
16. I believe that life is a battle to get my needs met.
17. I believe that God is in a good mood, and laughs.
18. I believe that God will punish me if I do wrong.
19. I believe that God sends people to hell.
20. I believe God considers me accepted, righteous, blessed and unconditionally loved.

After rating your beliefs, go to your journal with the three beliefs you feel need attention and do the exercise at the end of this chapter.

Power Truth # 2: It is Easy to Believe!

Don't throw rocks at me, but believing is easy. There, I said it, and now your wheels are turning and your past experiences are rising up, and the defenses are pulling out the shields and guns. Let me say it again; in fact, I am going to say it over and over again because that one lie that says believing or faith is hard is the root of many people's problems.

"But wait, you don't understand, I came from a rigid fundamentalist Pentecostal holiness apostolic second Baptist legalistic church of the end time order incorporated, and it took years for me to even start to get away from the guilt and shame."
I understand, but I have watched grown men get to chapters in one of my books and easily cry because the truth suddenly and easily took hold of their hearts.

It is easy to believe. You believe you can't get a good job, that you'll never be successful, that your life is always going to be this way, that your boss is a jerk, that your car is about to die, or that your family doesn't love you. That takes no effort whatsoever on your part does it? Good or bad, right or wrong, it is easy for you to believe those things. You do it every day.

Believing is easy. Some beliefs are unconscious, and programmed into daily life. Maybe it took a while for those beliefs to hold steady, and you may have persevered, but the believing is not hard. Even when you are gathering evidence to determine if you should believe something, the work of gathering evidence may be a challenge, but the believing isn't. You come to a place where the evidence is clear and then you make a choice to believe something. You choose to trust that something is true and you steadily adopt it. We start learning how to yield to a new belief.

Dr. Bruce Lipton, wrote a ground-breaking book called *The Biology of Belief* that really shook the world of biology. In the past, biologists believed that your genetics were set at conception and there wasn't anything you could do about it. They also believed that the cells of your body responded according to that set DNA. But Dr. Lipton discovered that the "brain" of every cell in your body is not in the nucleus of the cell, but on the outside. It opens to receive or to give off waste based on the information that is coming from outside the cell. It shuts down in a protection, fight-or-flight mode when danger is near. How does it know when danger is near? How do the cells of your body know when to be open and in a receiving mode? *Your cells actually respond to your beliefs.*

Your body also has divine principles built into it. In his book, *The Secret to Awesomeness*, Joshua Tongol says: *"Look, life forgives when you make mistakes, doesn't it? For instance, let's say you fall and scrape your knee or burn your hand from touching a hot stove. What happens afterward? You form new skin. Life takes what's wrong and makes it right again. In other words, it naturally gives your body a second chance"* (Kindle loc. 659). Even your own body believes in forgiveness.

So you were literally born a believer! It is the basic equipment that every person is born with and is woven into our very existence affecting everything about us. The way your body was created and the way that it functions from beliefs makes that clear.

In the Bible the followers of Christ were called believers. The word "Christian" is only used 3 times in the Bible, but the New International Version uses the word *believers* some 59 times! Even not trusting God is to believe in something or someone else. Everyone is a believer at heart!

That is why it's easy to believe. We do it every day in hundreds of ways. It's why you have been given the authority to *guard your own heart, for out of it flow the issues of life*......because you have the power to do so. Which brings me to...

Heart Truth 5—The Heart Is the Place from Which We Believe.

Did you know God empowers the heart to believe the truth. Moses' Law could tell you to not steal but it could not make you generous. It could say don't commit adultery but it couldn't make you love your spouse from your heart. The Law could forbid bearing false witness, but it did not make us honest at heart. God is not trying to get you to believe in the Ten Commandments, but to trust in what James called the *Royal Law of Love*.

So the problem is not even belief; the problem is *focus*. At our house, we have Dish as our satellite provider. At the beginning the installer came to the house and put a satellite dish at the top right corner of our house. Why? Because out in space is a satellite that is broadcasting a picture through an invisible signal. That signal requires a receiver to be pointed right at it. If there are no pictures or sound on the TV, it is not because the signal is bad. It is because the dish isn't pointed in the right direction.

We don't have a belief problem as much as we have a focus problem. *Turn your eyes upon Jesus, look full in His wonderful face, and the things of earth will grow strangely dim, in the light of His glory and grace!*

All He is asking from you is to turn the "satellite" dish of your heart toward God's love. Your ace in the hole is that God will be the author of your faith in the area where your beliefs need to change. No pastor, teacher, or preacher is the author of our faith. Look at the commitment God has to helping your heart:

JESUS - *"Looking unto Jesus, the AUTHOR and FINISHER of our FAITH..."* (Heb. 12:1). If you start noticing, you will find him initiating signs, events, situations, and affirmations of the new belief you are trying to embrace.

The FATHER - A group of people asked Jesus how to do the works of God, and Jesus answered and said to them, *"God wants to do something for you so that you believe in the one whom He has sent."* (John 6:29) Do you see God is the one who wants to do things in your life to help you believe the very best?

The SPIRIT - *"And since we have the same SPIRIT of FAITH, according to what is written, "I believed and therefore I spoke," we also believe and therefore speak."* (2 Cor. 4:13) Paul also wrote, *"But the fruit of the SPIRIT is* *love, joy, peace, longsuffering, gentleness, goodness, FAITH..."* (Gal. 5:22, KJV)

IMPORTANT NOTE: Our beliefs were rooted into our hearts usually by an experience. Experiences wire our brains and write on our hearts. So we need new God initiated experiences to re-wire and re-write healthy beliefs. Keep this in mind throughout the book and ask for them continually! The Bible doesn't say the truth will set you free. It says *knowing* the truth (which means by experience) will set you free!

You will release your inner awesome when your beliefs are not limitations, but are open doors through which love flows. Allow your beliefs to change and you allow your life to change. Then if you will watch closely you will begin to see evidences from God in which He is encouraging you onward in your dream.

Therefore, if any belief in your heart is inconsistent with love, it is your duty to allow it to be changed for out of the heart flow all the issues of life. Our heart beliefs are like filters for what can come out of our hearts. Even though the treasure of love's glorious *dunamis-power* is within us, our beliefs can quench it from flowing through us.

"Doubting Your Doubts" Exercise
Purpose: to challenge and dismantle limiting beliefs about your dream

In each chapter we are layering in the exercises with new pieces, not abandoning the previous ones. So have your journal handy.

What beliefs do you think are hindering you from your dream? For example, *"I'm too old; I'm not smart enough; things just don't go my way; I don't have enough money..."* Or what Global

Governing God Belief seems to be limiting you? Pick one limiting belief that you struggle with. Write it down:

I struggle with the belief that I am (or God is) _____.

As you learned in the previous exercise, when we pay attention to what is going on in the *now*, and notice without judging everything, we will naturally find ourselves in the present moment. The present is where God is.

As you breathe in, use your breath prayer... "Yah"... "weh". "I am"... "that I am." So close your eyes, put your hand over your heart, breathe in through your nose and out through your mouth in slow natural rhythms repeating the affirmation and awareness prayer. Continue until your heart is at rest in the present moment.

Use your breath prayer or this noticing exercise.

Simply notice things. Don't judge them as good or bad. Don't figure out a plan to change them. Simply notice without allowing your heart to evaluate and judge.

Breathe in through your nose and out through your mouth. Notice the way the air feels coming into your body and going back out again. With each breath pay attention to how it makes your body feel. Now notice the clothes that you are wearing. How do they feel on your body? Where do they move as you breathe in and out? What about your skin? Do you feel the temperature in the room? Notice the temperature of the air on your skin. What do you hear? Simply discern the variety of sounds all around you.

All these things are happening in the now. This is where you are. This is where God dwells. The *I Am* is now. As you sit in His presence, He is with you. He is for you. He loves you.

1. Take a moment and be thankful for love. Drink it in for a few minutes.

2. Now take out your journal again and ask yourself these questions:

> A. Can I know with 100% absolute certainty that this negative/limiting belief I have is true?
>
> Why might it not be true? Write down any and everything that comes to mind.
>
> B. Is it at all possible that there are other scriptures or understandings of God that I have not considered or been made aware of? Is it possible that God may want to change this belief? Yes or no?

3. Next, write down the opposite of that negative belief. For example, if it is "I am a victim of what others have done to me", write the opposite, "I am powerful to make life changing choices".

4. Once you write that positively do a "heart-belief buster". This means use your journal to write down in short ideas and statements any thoughts that come to you when you say that statement positively. It may take 10 minutes to allow all the thoughts, positive and negative to come out of the darkness of your heart into the light. Don't judge them, just write… and your perspective will softly change.

Let's say you wrote, "I am powerful to make life changing choices." You might write down, "I didn't feel powerful when I was abused as a child." "It seems like nothing ever changes, including me." "I did have the power to chose my response to the things that happened to me." Once you have exhausted any and all thoughts, you are done. By itself, simply bringing them to the light will often dispel the negative beliefs.

5. What would my life look like if this positive belief was true? Write it down.

6. Prayer: "Father I want to acknowledge every good thing that is in me by Christ Jesus and acknowledge every good thing about You. Since I need this new belief established in my heart, supply faith to me with evidences, encouragement and signs that it is true."

7. Now sit in His presence in the present with any residual negative emotions and just let them pass through you. Ask God to cleanse your heart with His life, love and light. Rest in that moment like you are simply watching it happen until you sense release and peace.

8. Make your way through the beliefs that you think are limiting you using the same principle. There will be more tools later, but start here.

PART 2

WHO AM I?

Who Am I? I Belong!

"Belonging is the safe place every heart longs for."

You belong! Will you believe that? You are accepted into a family. You may feel rejected, but "Rejected" is not your name! It's not the truth about you. It is not your identity! You belong! Love has included you in a family.

When I was five years old, my father sat me down at his new girlfriend's house and said he wanted to ask me a question. To an adult it seems rather innocuous, but from the processing capabilities of a child, it was a terrifying question. He said, "Do you want to live with me or with your mother after the divorce?" In my heart I interpreted the question as, "Which parent will you chose to love you? Which one will you belong to? If I chose one, I will not be loved by the other." That fear of not belonging, held its grip in my heart for decades causing me to either hold too tightly, or not care at all about people, neither of which were healthy options.

As long as I found my belonging in a group, a denomination, or a list of fundamentals, I was limited in my destiny. Once I began to really see that I belong to the family of Father, Son and Spirit, I was free to begin letting go of anything that was inconsistent with that love.

Abraham Maslow's hierarchy of needs demonstrated that a sense of belonging is fundamental to human fulfillment, personal growth and happiness. For example, for many if there is a time when the sense of belonging feels stripped away, it is in the painful context of divorce. The divorced person feels like he or she doesn't belong in the family unit anymore. Then sometimes friends are afraid to choose sides in a situation and don't know what to say so they tend to withdraw. Before long, the loss of belonging feels devastating.

Ryan C. Jones, in his Doctor of Philosophy dissertation at Oklahoma State University, also showed that the loss of a sense of belonging is one of the greatest predictors of depression and has been shown to affect our emotional and physical health, our ability to concentrate and our ability to cope with life changes.

I recently watched a *Ted Talks* on YouTube by British Journalist, Johann Hari, called "Everything You Think You Know About Addiction is Wrong". Because he grew up in a family of addicts and wanted to also help his friends get out of addiction, Johann started on a journey of trying to understand why our modern addiction recovery programs really don't work. He discovered that the morphine that is given to patients undergoing surgery in a hospital tend to NOT become addictive even though it is the equivalent of pure, uncut heroin, yet impure street heroin is very watered down in its potency. If it was the drug itself then many people would be addicted after coming home from surgery.

On the other hand, a Professor of Psychology in Vancouver re-examined the experiment from the 70's which put a rat in a cage with a bottle of water, and a bottle with heroin in it. The original experiment said that the rat would crave the drug and even take it until it overdosed. But this new researcher did something different. He wondered if the environment would affect the rat's choices. So he created a Rat Park Wonderland where the rat had other rats, cheese, tunnels, food, fun things to do and all the sex it wanted.

What they found was astounding. The rats rarely used the heroin and never overdosed...because of connection, belonging, and purpose, whereas the other experiment brought isolation, disconnection and a lack of purpose.

He then said that Portugal had one of the highest drug addiction rates on the planet. It was so bad that the government pulled together a panel to discover what could be done. Eventually, they decided to get rid of all drug laws so that heroin, cannabis, cocaine, etc., were all legal. But the catch was that they would take the money they were spending on the "drug war" and use it to help addicts to connect. For instance, they would take a convicted addict to a business and say, "If you will hire this guy, we will pay half his salary for a year."

Do you know what happened? Drug addiction declined by 50%.

What does that tell us about ourselves? We need *connection*, *belonging* and *purpose* if we are to fulfill our desires. Otherwise we could be wasting life energy trying to obtain something that we already possess but didn't know it!

Let's transform and transition Johann Hari's idea a bit and explore the place of your belonging. Go back with me before there was religion of any kind, before societies sprang forth, before the Garden of Eden, before there were stars in the sky or trees in the field. Take a leap back before creation itself. What do we find there? We find Father, Son and Holy Spirit in eternal communion.

The origin of belonging isn't in a golf club, a caste system or hanging with the hipsters. The origin of all belonging is found in the concept from which it emerged. All belonging comes from the nature of God. Did you know God's nature is community and belonging? God always existed in community where the Father delighted in the Son, and the Spirit honored the Father, and the Son loved the Father and so on. The Trinity enjoyed mutual relationships of intense joy, perfect love, and peace beyond our comprehension.

So perfect was the communion, the interaction and connectedness that all creation came out of the desire for us to experience what Father, Son and Spirit enjoy in one another. It was God's intention from the beginning to bring us into that circle of belonging. So ***this grace was given us in Christ Jesus <u>before</u> the beginning of time,*** (2 Timothy 1:9).

John echos this saying, *"**That which was from the beginning**, which we have heard, which we have seen with our eyes, which we have looked upon, and our hands have handled, concerning the Word of life— **the life was manifested**, and we have seen, and bear witness, and declare to you that eternal life which was **with the Father and was manifested to us**— that which we have seen and heard we declare to you, that you also may have fellowship with us; and truly **our fellowship is with the Father and with His Son** Jesus Christ."* (1 John 1:1-3).

The word fellowship is the word communion or sharing. This belonging was **the life** of communion, sharing, fellowship that always existed between Father and Son. John saw with his own eyes the relationship Jesus had with the Father and Spirit. Jesus as the Son of Man included you in His death, His burial, resurrection and ascension in order to seat you *together with him in the heavenly places. You died and your life is hidden with Christ in God.* Being in Christ means that we don't need to wait until we die to relish the joy that the Father has for us.

In other words, it is as if we are so standing inside heaven's

Trinity that Jesus said the Father loves us the same profound way that he loves the Son (John 17:23). The way the Spirit honors the Father is how the Spirit honors you. The delight the Son has for the Father is the same delight he has for you! Take a moment to imagine that truth!

Do you remember the story of the **lost coin**, the **lost sheep** and the **lost son** in Luke 15? By giving them these titles, the translators missed an important truth. They are really about the seeking, compassionate and lavish God and his relationship with "lost" things. Each story tells of something that was lost and the one who was looking intently for it.

The woman who lost the coin searched for it because it was still of value. She searched until it was found. It wasn't the woman who needed to be found, it was the coin. The good shepherd rescued the lost sheep from having wandered from the fold. The father was already looking and watching for the son and in seeing him, he ran toward, and kissed the son repeatedly. He then restored what was wasted and threw a party! In fact, other than the older son, the only one not happy about the son returning was the fatted calf!

What is often overlooked is this: how could the coin be lost if it did not belong to begin with? Did she steal it? What right did the shepherd have to take up the sheep on his shoulders if it didn't belong to him? That would make him a thief wouldn't it? Even though the son was thought to be dead, the father never quit considering him to be his son. He was always a son. Just because he was *lost*, didn't mean he didn't still *belong*.

<u>You belong before you believe</u>. You belong before you see that you belong. It is simply that we were in the darkness of not understanding. The Gospel is not a declaration that you are accepted after you get your life together. It is the message that you, through Christ, are accepted now along with the invitation to believe it, so that you can experience all the sense of belonging that God intended for you to have from the beginning. *You don't believe something in order to make it true. You believe it because it **is** already true.* Then the Spirit bears witness with your spirit that you are a child of God.

That's why Paul said in Ephesians 4:6, ***"one God and Father of all, who is over all, and through all, and in all."*** You belong to your Father in heaven. Home isn't a building made of wood and brick. Your home is in the heart of God, in the family of God. Ephesians 3:15 says, ***"from whom the whole family in heaven and earth is named."***

"Then where was God when I needed Him?" Did you know that there are some things that God can't do? He won't violate our free will. He will not violate love. Sometimes in a bad marriage, we are begging Him to change the other person, to make the court judge work on our behalf but God will not force someone to do His will or our will. He will not violate love or free will.

One might say, *"So then where was he when my career crashed and my marriage failed?"* He was with you and is still with you today. That is why one of the primary prayers we are to pray is for wisdom because generally what we want is use God like a product that we pay for. We make our "prayer payment" and He has to fix everybody and everything. If it doesn't happen, then we pray longer and louder thinking that makes a difference, instead of praying for wisdom in which we receive direction to navigate *through* things! Sometimes we are afraid of the direction He is giving us so we compound our problems and then blame God because He didn't fix it. But you were never alone.

God didn't "allow" that to happen to you. He didn't put you through something to teach you a lesson, though we can certainly learn lessons from it. It was simply a convergence of your decisions and/or someone else's decisions. In a bad marriage, for instance, hearts get hard and things happen. What God can do, no matter what happens, He will work all things together for your good. That is why we have to look for his goodness. Every single day He is bringing good into our lives, if we are training our heart to see it again.

You have never been alone...ever. *He is a very PRESENT help in time of need.*

Here is one of life's greatest discoveries. Jesus said in John 14:20, *"In that day you will know that I am in My Father, and you in Me, and I am in you."* Paul found this to be true in Galatians 1:15-16, *"But when it pleased God, who separated me from my mother's womb and called me through His grace, to reveal His Son in me, that I might preach Him among the Gentiles, I did not immediately confer with flesh and blood......"* Did you catch that? It was not just that God revealed His Son *to* Paul—that is true—but He revealed His Son IN HIM! He is SO present with you......not simply like a friend walking beside you, but He is IN you.

This journey of living and loving your dream begins with learning to believe that you belong in the family and are part of a family business. Out of that you can discover purpose for your life. You are so well connected! God is present with you forever to give wisdom, counsel, direction, comfort and companionship.

The Identity Exercise
Purpose: to begin establishing a sense of belonging

Imagine that your whole body is a filter and when you breathe in you are breathing air not through your nose but through your entire body all at the same time. So close your eyes, put your hand over your heart, breathe in through your nose and out through your mouth in slow natural rhythms. Allow your stomach to rise and fall naturally.

As you learned in the previous exercise, when we pay attention to what is going on in the now, and notice without judging everything, we will find ourselves in the present moment. The present is where God is. As you breathe in imagine you are breathing in wisdom, or truth, or glory, and as you breathe out imagine it all coming back out of you into the world around you.

Simply notice things. Don't judge them as good or bad. Don't figure out a plan to change them. Simply notice.

Breathe in through your nose and out through your mouth. Notice the way the air feel coming into your body and going back out again. With each breath pay attention to how it makes your body feel. Now notice the clothes that you are wearing. How do they feel on your body? Where do they move as you breathe in and out? What about your skin? Do you feel the temperature in the room? Notice the temperature of the air on your skin. What do you hear? Simply discern the variety of sounds all around you.

All these things are happening in the now. This is where you are. This is where God dwells. The I Am. As you sit in His presence, He is with you; He is for you; He loves you.

1. Take a moment and be thankful for love. Drink it in for a few minutes.

2. Now take out your journal again and ask yourself these questions:

> A. Can I know with 100% absolute certainty that this negative/limiting belief I have is true?
>
> Why might it not be true? Write down any and everything that comes to mind.
>
> B. Is it at all possible that there are other scriptures or understandings of God that I have not considered or been made aware of? Is it possible that God may want to change this belief? Yes or no?

3. Next, write down the opposite of that negative belief. For example, if it is "I never felt like I belonged anywhere or to anyone", write some opposite, "I belong to the Father, Son and Holy Spirit and to the human family."

4. Once you write that positively do a "heart-belief buster". This means use your journal to write down in short ideas and statements any thoughts that come to you when you say that statement positively. It may take 10 minutes to allow all the thoughts, positive and negative, to come out of the darkness of your heart into the light. Don't judge them, just write… and your perspective will softly change.

Let's say you wrote, "I belong to the Father, Son and Holy Spirit and to the human family." You might write down, "I never felt like I belonged because I was different." "My family didn't tell me that or treat me that way though." "Maybe I picked that up at school." "Since my family didn't teach me, I used to feel belonging there." "I remember what that felt like.." Once you have exhausted any and all thoughts, you are done. By itself, simply bringing them to the light will often dispel the negative beliefs.

5. What would my life look like if this positive belief was true? Write it down.

6. Prayer: "Father I want to acknowledge every good thing that is in me by Christ Jesus and acknowledge every good thing about You. Since I need this new belief established in my heart, supply faith to me with evidences, encouragement and signs that it is true."

7. Now sit in His presence in the present with any residual negative emotions and just let them pass through you. Ask God to cleanse your heart with His life, love and light. Rest in that moment like you are simply watching it happen until you sense release and peace.

Who Am I? I Am Worthy

"Self-worth comes from one thing - the value God has placed on your life."
-Chuck Crisco

Are you one of those people who struggle with self-worth? Do you tend to compare yourself with others? *"Mike always gets the better hand." "Angela was born into money and I wasn't, therefore I can't have the life she has."*

Do you apologize for practically everything saying in your heart, *"I'm sorry for being alive!"*?

Do you take the default position that you must be wrong? You are always telling others, *"You're right."*

Do you regularly avoid eye contact with others... even those who love you?

Do you rarely ask for what you want?

How well do you handle compliments and affirmation? Do you deflect them or do you embrace them?

Do you obsessively avoid failure and try to appear perfect to others? This, of course, results in lots of "white lies" doesn't it?

How do you measure your value? How important are you in your *own* eyes?

Jesus said, *"Judge not"*. Paul said, *"I don't even judge my own life."* Yet most of us have an arbitrary standard by which we are judging our worth. Maybe you are comparing yourself to the apostles, or to a spiritual leader, or to someone who has been successful. It is incredibly wise to learn from them, but never to compare to them. Maybe you are comparing yourself with the Law. Maybe you are comparing yourself with the perfection of Christ.

In fact, notice what it says in Acts 13:46, *"Then Paul and Barnabas spoke out boldly and declared, 'It was necessary that we first preach the word of God to you Jews. But since you have rejected it and judged yourselves unworthy of eternal life, we will offer it to the Gentiles.'"* God did not judge them unworthy. They judged themselves that way and missed the life God was promising them. Your worth, your value can only be defined by the One who created you, or by how much one is willing to give to have a relationship with you.

I heard a great illustration once. A conference speaker held up a $500 dollar bill. He said, "How many of you would like this?" Everyone raised their hands. Then he took it and crumpled it up and said, "How many of you want this now?" Still all the hands were raised. Then once more he took it and put it on the floor under his dirty shoe and dirtied it. Then he said, "Now how many of you want it?" Still everyone raised their hands. So the said, "Today you learned a valuable lesson. You still wanted it, because even though it was crumpled, even though it was dirty, it was *still* worth $500." So, too, is your life.

See, God's perspective is the only one that really counts. He says that even though you felt broken, crumpled, and dirty, He saw the value of who you were anyway. You didn't lose your value to

God. Some people see their contribution to the world as worthless because they believe they are worthless in their heart.

If I go out to a nice restaurant and pay $75 for a meal, it is because I already made up my mind that it was worth it to me. I paid the price according to the value of the meal. How much did Jesus give for you? You are worth the blood of Jesus!!! 1 Peter 1:18-19 says, *"knowing that you were not redeemed with perishable things like silver or gold from your futile way of life inherited from your forefathers, but with precious blood, as of a lamb unblemished and spotless, the blood of Christ...."*

Not only that, but Romans 6:11 says, *"Consider yourselves dead indeed to sin, and your relation to it broken, but alive to God in unbroken fellowship."* (AMP) If you count or consider yourself outside of what Christ has done or what Christ has said about you then you will end up with the wrong conclusion. How long have you been using the wrong formula to arrive at your value? We are to consider that we are in an eternal relationship where God never breaks fellowship with us!

Paul said **we are not to compare ourselves one to another because it isn't wise.** So instead of comparing yourself with Christ, you are to find yourself IN Christ. You must locate yourself there or end up with the wrong definition of who you are. *Whatever is true of Jesus is true of you in Christ.* He valued you so much that in the incarnation He became the Son of Man, not only to deal with sin but to bring you into unbroken fellowship with the Father. Jesus isn't the way to heaven; He is the way to the Father. He has seated you together with Himself on the throne of grace. He has brought you into the communion of the Father, Son and Spirit.

So the reason you are worthy is based on the objective fact that

God demonstrated it for all to see!

The Identity Exercise
Purpose: to begin establishing a sense of worth

Imagine that your whole body is a filter and when you breathe in you are breathing air not through your nose but through your entire body all at the same time. Allow your stomach to rise and fall naturally. Close your eyes, put your hand over your heart, breathe in through your nose and out through your mouth in slow natural rhythms.

As you learned in the previous exercise, when we pay attention to what is going on in the now, and notice without judging everything, we will find ourselves in the present moment. The present is where God is. As you breathe in imagine you are breathing in wisdom, or truth or glory, and as you breathe out imagine it all coming back out of you into the world around you. Or use the "breath prayer", "Yah…weh. I am… that I am."

Simply notice things. Don't judge them as good or bad. Don't figure out a plan to change them. Simply notice.

Breathe in through your nose and out through your mouth. Notice the way the air feels coming into your body and going back out again. With each breath pay attention to how it makes your body feel. Now, notice the clothes that you are wearing. How do they feel on your body? Where do they move as you breathe in and out? What about your skin? Do you feel the temperature in the room? Notice the temperature of the air on your skin. What do you hear? Simply discern the variety of sounds all around you.

All these things are happening in the now. This is where you are.

This is where God dwells. The **I Am**. As you sit in His presence, He is with you; He is for you; He loves you.

1. Take a moment and be thankful for love. Drink it in for a few minutes.

2. Now take out your journal again and ask yourself these questions:

> **A.** Can I know with 100% absolute certainty that this negative/limiting belief I have is true?
>
> Why might it not be true? Write down any and everything that comes to mind.
>
> **B.** Is it at all possible that there are other scriptures or understandings of God that I have not considered or been made aware of? Is it possible that God may want to change this belief? Yes or no?

3. Next, write down the opposite of that negative belief. For example, if it is "I feel unworthy for good things", write the opposite, "I am a valuable and worthy person."

4. Once you write that positively do a "heart-belief buster". This means use your journal to write down in short ideas and statements any thoughts that come to you when you say that statement positively. It may take 10 minutes to allow all the thoughts, positive and negative, to come out of the darkness of your heart into the light. Don't judge them, just write… and your perspective will softly change.

5. What would my life look like if this positive belief was true? Write it down.

6. Prayer: "Father I want to acknowledge every good thing that is in me by Christ Jesus and every good thing about You. Since I need this new belief established in my heart, supply faith to me with evidences, encouragement and signs that it is true."

7. Now sit in His presence in the present with any residual negative emotions and just let them pass through you. Ask God to cleanse your heart with His life, love and light. Rest in that moment like you are simply watching it happen until you sense release and peace.

PART 3

UNCOVERING YOUR DREAM:
Destiny Discovery

You Have GRACE for Failure...And PERMISSION For Success!

"Our greatest fear should not be of failure, but of succeeding at things in life that don't really matter."
–Francis Chan

If God is for you, who can be against you? He, along with the great cloud of witnesses, never stops cheering you on, even when you fail or make mistakes. There is no greater limitation on our lives than the belief that God is limiting us, for how could one escape that? Try to be perfect? Well, Christ has done that on my behalf already. It is called the gift of righteousness. Bargain with Him that I will give him my whole life? Well, everything already belongs to Him.

Your success is of the greatest importance to Him. So much so that you are blessed with every spiritual blessing in the heavenly places. Do you know what "blessing" is? It is not a check for $100 you get in the mail and call it a blessing. That is the result of blessing, but it, in and of itself, is not the blessing. The blessing is the empowerment of God to prosper. It is the favor of God to succeed. It is the Spirit making you fruitful in every good work and blessing the work of your hands.

What if you could not ultimately fail in any endeavor? What would your one genie wish be? What would you ask to be empowered with for the rest of your life, if no matter what happened it would not be a failure?

Success, is to live your life from your spirit as the most authentic person you can be; THEN all the other stuff will come out of that.

Do you realize that God has so guaranteed your success that He has promised to work all things together for your good? In fact, because where sin abounds grace does much more abound, there is no such thing as failure, ultimately.

But what about the early Church selling their property in Jerusalem and sharing it with each other out of the spirit of generosity? What about Jesus telling them to leave their houses and lands to follow him? Was this evidence that God had no intention of prospering them; that we are all destined for poverty? Was he promising them failure?

On the contrary, it was one of the most incredible prophetic words of wealth-building and success that you can imagine. It was real generosity coming from a recognition that many of us miss. They had a prophetic word from Jesus that Jerusalem was going to be destroyed within one generation from the time of the cross. Exactly 40 years later, in AD 70 the city was destroyed and all the possessions within it were either burned or plundered. God's purpose was for them to prosper in every way so he gave them a wisdom strategy ahead of time: sell now and provide for each other.

Now let's look at a powerful story that will be your trump card no matter what happens! In order to succeed you need to *let go of your fear of failure as being fatal.*

In Luke 22:31-34, the Lord said, *"Simon, Simon! Indeed, Satan has asked for you, that he may sift you as wheat. But I have prayed for you, that your faith should not fail; and when you have returned to Me, strengthen your brethren." But he said to*

Him, "Lord, I am ready to go with You, both to prison and to death." Then He said, "I tell you, Peter, the rooster shall not crow this day before you will deny three times that you know Me."

Jesus Was NOT OFFENDED at Him or What He Was About Do.

Let that simmer for a minute. I'm not saying that He endorsed his behavior. It was a huge deal. Peter betrayed his best Friend. Peter denied Jesus. Peter abandoned Him in His crucial hour. But come a little closer. There is no hint that Jesus was angry either before, during or after. He wasn't offended at his sin. Remember, Jesus said, ***"If you have seen Me you have seen the Father."*** Jesus was the exact representation of the Father. Whatever you see Jesus doing, it's because the Father is doing it. Jesus wasn't endorsing bad behavior, but neither was He offended. That means the Father wasn't either! You can never separate the two.

Jesus said He and the Father are one. Not two opinions, or two views, but one! Jesus wasn't on the cross saying, "Father, You'd better do something here or I'm gonna kill them!" There is always perfect harmony.

I have a friend in the Nashville area who was the pastor of a church that began to experience a time of powerful "revival" and amazing miracles. But then he started having some problems in his marriage, and when the marriage fell apart so did the church and his life. At one point he was sleeping in an abandoned church and an old woman next door would let him wash off with the hose outside.

But do you know what? God never left his side, never quit

loving him and never abandoned him. He would be in a bar getting drunk, and people would randomly encourage him as a child of God. One night he picked up a girl, and in the very act of sex, she starts to speak in tongues and he gets the interpretation of God saying "I love you, this is not who you really are!" Can you imagine?! God is love and wasn't operating in offense. God's love for you is patient and kind. God's love keeps no record of wrongs…it does not take account of a wrong suffered.

Jesus Did Not Even PRAY About His Behavior.

Why? Do you realize that Jesus knew Peter was about to deny him, yet Jesus did *not* tell him, *"Peter, I have prayed for you that you sin not."* He knew he would sin. He knew he was going to sin big, and He knew that there wasn't a prayer He could pray that was going to keep Peter from his sin. Have we made sin bigger than the love of God, the grace of God, and the blood of Jesus?

He prayed for him that his FAITH would not fail. He prayed for him that Peter, in the end, would not lose his confidence in Jesus. He's not problem-focused, he is solution-focused! Jesus is praying for you that your FAITH will fail not; because when you see Him clearly you will not run *from* God in your failures, you will run *to* Him. He's not minimizing our poor choices. He knows that when mistakes encounter His love, guilt doesn't have a chance!

Jesus Forgave Peter BEFORE Peter Received It.

Don't run from this. Stare it down face-to-face with the revelation of the Father. Let the story teach you the nature and ministry of the Gospel! In Matthew it says, *"After you are restored, strengthen your brothers, and I'll meet you in Galilee"* (the place by the Sea where He restored Peter). Forgiveness <u>always</u> precedes the reception of it. Someone will say, *"If you start telling people that, they are going to use it as an excuse for sin."* Friends, I promise you, people don't need an excuse. They do what they want because they want to. The problem is that they don't have a safe God to run to *afterwards* who loves them in spite of it! Failures of any kind are not fatal unless you allow them to affect you permanently.

Matthew 9 tells the story of how some friends of a paralyzed man brought him to Jesus. It says that Jesus *"saw their faith"*. It was the confidence of the four men who brought him. Seeing their faith Jesus said, "Rise and walk, right"? No. Before the paralyzed man confessed a sin...before he did any act of repentance or penance...before he said a sinner's prayer, Jesus said, *"Son, your sins are forgiven!"*

The religious people said, "Wait, who do you think you are when only God has the authority to forgive sin?" Their misunderstanding is our revelation truth! Yes, that's right, the Father gave the Son the right to forgive him before any action or request on the paralyzed man's part.

That's why it says in Acts 13:38, *"Let it be known to you, therefore, brothers, that through this Man, forgiveness of sins is proclaimed to you!"* We are not trying to get people to follow a religion and qualify for it by being good people. Christ comes to you to declare that you are forgiven. Now change your mind about God (repent) and trust it.

But wait, doesn't John say, *"If we confess our sins He is faithful and just to forgive us our sins and cleanse us of all unrighteousness."*? Yes, it does. But He is *not* making a decision

81

to pardon based on your confession. Do you know what the word *confess* means? It literally means *to say the same thing as*. It means that you are saying the same thing about sin that God does! Forgiven! Did you know what the word *forgive* is there in Greek? It simply means *to send away* not *pardon*. God already took away the sin of the world. So it means that He comes to cleanse *us* by sending guilt away from our heart.

Peter Do You Love Me?

At the end of John's Gospel, we read the story about how Jesus restored Peter three times by saying to him, ***"Peter do you love me?" "Yes, Lord, You know I love you." "Then feed My sheep."*** Why? Because He was trying to teach Peter that he really did love Jesus, but he was not to trust in how much *Peter* loved *Jesus*; instead, he was to trust in how much *Jesus* loved *Peter*. At his very best, Peter wanted to wash Jesus' feet, but Jesus washed *Peter's* feet. Peter promised to never deny Him, but it was Jesus who didn't deny Peter. Peter promised to die for Him, but it was *Jesus* who died for *Peter*!

Yet Peter utterly failed at every turn. That's because Peter always had it backwards and upside-down. For Peter, and all those who live under legalism, they see themselves as the ones who must do good for God to be a good Christian. They see *themselves* as the source. That is why Jesus said that to *"love the Lord your God with all your heart, mind, soul, and strength..."* was the fulfillment of the Law's expectation. But that is not how the New Covenant works. In the New Covenant, Jesus said, *"love one another as I have loved you."* That makes HIM the source of all love, instead of us.

In the Upper Room, Jesus said, ***"A new commandment I give you that you love one another as I have loved you."*** That word *new* is **kainos**, meaning *brand new; we haven't done it like this before.* Loving God with all your heart in order to please God and be right with God made us the source, and we could never do it. Peter could never pull it off.

THIS GOD IS NOT OFFENDED AT YOUR FAILURES. HE IS INTERCEDING FOR YOUR DUNAMIS-ABILITY TO SEE HIS GOODNESS. HE IS SUPPLYING FAITH, NOT DEMANDING IT, AND HE FORGIVES YOU BEFORE YOU ASK!

God has empowered you, blessed you to prosper in that which is worthwhile, but He has also given you a safety net. It is the certainty that if you fail, no matter how bad you fail, God is not offended; Jesus is interceding that you will see Him and His love, and set you right back on course. You have the grace in the midst of failures of any kind so that it won't be fatal. In the heart of God He has also given you permission to succeed.

To succeed in what matters, don't allow failure to define you. Accept love and move on. People can encourage you, but you have to take responsibility to not allow God's love to go to waste in your life!

Radical Prayer Exercise
Purpose: to trust Christ's ability to reveal his love to you

Your desire may face a contradiction from time to time. There may be obstacles to overcome. You may even fail along the way. So now, at this point in your journey of learning to live and love the life of your dreams here is a suggested prayer:

"Father I thank You for forgiveness for my failures and

permission to succeed. I am thankful *I am not on a probation period with You.* Father I thank you that my faith will fail not because I trust that I will grow in seeing You for who you are, and for seeing myself in light of Your love."

Where Am I Going? Follow Your Bliss

As the Cheshire cat asked Alice in Wonderland,
"Would you tell me, please, which way I ought to go from here?"
"That depends a good deal on where you want to get to."
"I don't much care where –"
"Then it doesn't matter which way you go."
—Lewis Carroll, *Alice in Wonderland*

That is the way most people live their lives. They aren't really honoring their true selves and they simply wait until life unfolds with no direction, no planning, no sense of outward purpose. Living in spiritual rest doesn't mean living a life without direction.

Need direction? Try Following Your Bliss!

There is a famous quote by Joseph Campbell that inspires me! *"Follow your bliss. If you do follow your bliss, you put yourself on a kind of track that has been there all the while waiting for you, and the life you ought to be living is the one you are living...When you can see that, you begin to meet people who are in the field of your bliss, and they open the doors to you. I say, follow your bliss and don't be afraid, and doors will open where you didn't know they were going to be. If you follow your bliss, doors will open for you that wouldn't have opened for anyone else."*

Who are you? You are a spiritual-soul being living in a human body. But you aren't just any spiritual being. YOU have been united to Christ's Spirit. You have become the Holy of Holies for God, Himself. The real you, the *you* that is the essence of you is not God, but your spirit has been made divine by your union with the Spirit of Christ. That is why YOU, the real YOU is righteous. It's not just because He says it... it is because HE DID IT! Bliss is an inside job!

The Path of Bliss

One of the main signs that you are *not* headed in the right direction is depression. I'm not saying every experience of depression is the same, but one of the signs that you are headed in the wrong direction can be a sense of depression. It means that WHAT is in you, and WHO is in you and what you are DOING with your life are not synchronized! There is a sense of bliss when what is inside of you is lined up with what you are doing with your life.

I want to challenge you to follow your bliss! Follow your spiritual joy—that which you love to do, that which you deeply enjoy, that which motivates you is not just you. It's God trying to line you up with your destiny!

As Dale Carnegie said, *"People rarely succeed unless they have fun in what they are doing."*

Or as someone once said, *"Choose a job you love, and you will never have to work a day in your life."* Follow your bliss! Did you know that God was trying to use the deep spiritual joy and bliss of your heart to lead you into your future? It is His "fishing hook" to draw you into expressing your unique design in Christ!

Isaiah 55:12, *"For you shall go out with joy, and be led out with peace; the mountains and the hills shall break forth into singing before you, and all the trees of the field shall clap their hands"*

(NAS).

Imagine standing in front of your little one-year-old as a parent while your precious baby tries to take his first hesitant steps. Are your arms folded taunting him, or are you cheering and celebrating with joy? Creation is singing your song, and clapping their hands inviting you into your destiny! Abba Daddy is cheering as His heart bursts with joy. Dirty diapers don't discourage him. As in the story of the prodigal son, follow the sound of heaven's party and keep walking!

We think that He leads us by an audible voice. I've heard Him like this several times in my life. I've heard a lot of whispers, too. Many think He leads with signs. I've been directed by these as well. But one of the primary ways is by stirring up joy in us to do something or enjoy something or someone, or some new way of life. Follow those intuitions.

Need More Proof?

Philippians 2:13, *"For it is God who works in you both to will and to do for His good pleasure (delight)." [Not in your own strength] for it is God Who is all the while effectually at work in you [energizing and creating in you the power and desire], both to will and to work for His good pleasure and satisfaction and delight"* (AMP).

Did you catch that? Do you know this is how God changes us, moves in us, works through us? It is not by demanding it from the outside but by motivating us from the inside. Sometimes when I don't know what to do I just say, *"God if this is a good path for me, I ask that you influence my heart, work in me so that what you want and what I want are the same thing."* And one of the ways he does that is by bliss.

I'm not talking about being led by destructive sinful pleasures. If you enjoy raping, pillaging and murdering, it's probably not God. (Lots of sarcasm intended!) That is why you present your heart to God for Him to fill it with His delight for the next step for your life!

I'm not even talking about following your excitement. Sometimes soulish excitement getting sucked into a sale on the Home Shopping Network, or suckered into buying that SUV that you can't afford. Next, you are kicking yourself with buyer's remorse and blaming God!

His desires start becoming your desires naturally because you are one with Him. It is rarely dramatic. Instead, it is the subtle reality of joy coming into your consciousness as lightly as a morning mist on the wings of a butterfly. The fact is that most of the time we ignore those pulls of joy and think God, for instance, would never want you to be wealthy because all money is sinful. Paul didn't say that money was the root of all evil. He said the *love* of money was the root of all *kinds* of evil. What if God actually wants you to be wealthy?

Step Ahead Even If It's Hard

That means start taking some steps in that direction. Be led by the Spirit's bliss. WARNING: *if you follow everything everybody else wants you to do you, will end up being conformed to THEIR image instead of the image of Christ for YOUR life.* No one else can walk your path.

Hebrews 12:2, ***"looking unto Jesus, the Author and Finisher of our faith, who for the joy that was set before Him endured the cross, despising the shame, and has sat down at the right*** *hand of the throne of God."*

It may be that following your bliss is hard because in the short run it is going to cost you something. That is what the author of Hebrews says. Jesus followed His bliss *through* the difficulties. So following your bliss doesn't mean that we bail out of things just because they are hard. But in the big picture, it is God who works in us to will and do of His good pleasure pointing you to your future. Follow your bliss!

Heart Truth 6—The Will of God is Found Inside Your Heart.

What is God's will for my life? How many people have asked that question? The problem is that it is the wrong question to ask. What??? Yes. First of all the Bible isn't going to tell you whether you should marry Susan or Mariah. It isn't going to tell you whether you should become an astronaut or an accountant. You aren't going to find those specific answers in the Bible.

In fact, most of the scriptures that speak about the will of God have to do with:

1) Jesus is the Father's will, the center of His affection, the height of His glory.

2) You are the will of God. He chose you and wanted you.

3) We are being conformed into His image. In other words, the will of God is for you to grow up into Christ, looking more like His love…for *your* benefit. The will of God is for you to love yourself, love people, and love life. It has very little to do with an absolute, predetermined direction for your life.

What about being *"led by the Spirit"*? The context of that passage from Romans 8 is not about Him saying "turn here" or "go there." The context says those who are led by the Spirit are creating personal evidence to themselves that they are sons of God by continually growing in leaving their false identity behind. They focus on being led into greater expressions of their true nature, or as Abraham Lincoln said, "the better angels of our nature."

Of course, God can speak to you and give you direction and wisdom for your life. He can give you a sense of outward purpose for your life. I am doing what I am doing today because God has directed me many times, but His "big picture" promises to me have never been inconsistent from my own heart's desires.

Not everyone gets a bright light encounter, though. That could be the lowest form of direction, because it means we are not listening to our heart. In fact, most of the time your sense of direction seems very natural. Paul said, *"It is God who works in us to will and do of His good pleasure."* And Psalm 37:4, *"Delight yourself also in the Lord and He will give you the desires of your heart."* So if it is in your heart, and it doesn't harm others, then go for it.

This is a yes and amen Gospel. All the promises of God are yes and amen. The will of God is not some mystery that he doles out in tiny glimpses based on our intense seeking. Unless you get a loud specific non fear-based "no!", it is always "yes" to love!

In Romans 12, Paul says do not be conformed to this world. We think that he is talking about "worldliness", but the Greek word there is actually "age". He was saying don't be conformed to the legalistic age of the Law that was fading away (Hebrews 8:13).

Instead we are to renew our minds and prove what is the good, acceptable and perfect will of God.

Was he teaching that God has a good will, an acceptable will, and then a perfect will. No, they are not concentric circles with each one being different. He is saying that the will of God is for us to be conformed to the image of Christ and overcome evil with good and live from love. Those things are good and acceptable to God and perfect, or mature expressions of His will.

The Source of Your Love:

Where do you think that your love for flying comes from? God loves flying. He created birds, so he knows a little bit about it. Where do you think that your love for farming, or riding bulls, or dancing comes from? It comes from God. Those are things that He delights in, things that He enjoys! God loves life, and as the Creator, He is inviting you into what HE loves! You are actually participating in the life that God enjoys. So take a clue from what you enjoy, and know that God is in it!

The only real *"directional"* scripture you are going to find in the Bible is when James said, *"Come now, you who say, 'Today or tomorrow we will go to such and such a city, spend a year there, buy and sell, and make a profit', whereas you do not know what will happen tomorrow. For what is your life? It is even a vapor that appears for a little time and then vanishes away. Instead, you ought to say, 'If the Lord wills, we shall live and do this or that'"* (James 4:3-15).

He isn't saying don't make any plans. Instead, He is saying to keep the attitude that the Lord can change your path and direction throughout your life. This happened to Paul when the Holy Spirit called him and Barnabas into a missionary journey.

What did they do? They took the steps and started out. They said "yes!" and figured it out as they went. As they traveled, the Holy Spirit forbade him to go into Bithynia and instead invited him to go to Macedonia. So you can get course corrections for your life because of God's love for you, thank God. But you GO first, get moving, take some steps forward and God will give you wisdom along the way. Say YES to love and to life!

See, the ***inner purpose*** of your life is to connect and manifest the real you that was created in love. That is an eternal unchanging purpose for your life. But the ***outward purpose*** for your life can change. You can't be a stunt man forever. You can't be a mother to your kids every day once they grow up and move out. Those outward purposes can be wonderful, but they can change. You may not be a pastor or lawyer forever, but you can be a a loving human being in whatever you do.

So follow your bliss, your inner joy, even if it takes time and you need more education, training, or experience. Follow your bliss, even if you need to start a side business to support that vision. The will of God for your life will come from within, and it will feel like *you* because the will of God for you is to be like Jesus (love) and to follow your spirit.

If you are waiting for Him to tell you what to do, He is doing that right now by asking, *"What do YOU want to do? Go for it, and I am empowering you to succeed!"*

I think we all want to make some kind of impact in the world. We all want to leave a legacy. We all want to leave our footprints on the moon. We all want our lives to have purpose and meaning. But how?

Notice what Paul said in 1 Corinthians 15:45, ***"the first Adam*** *became a living being, but the last Adam became a life-giving spirit"* (NIV). Jesus Christ, the Last Adam, became a life-giving spirit in His ascension. Do you want to live the abundant life of Christ? Do you want to make some small difference in the world? The life-giving Spirit has purposed to flow through you. Christ wants the increase of His love in the earth... but he does it through leading us by making His delight, our delight! God works in us to will and do of His good pleasure, and when you yield to your bliss, you give Christ's life to the world around you!

The Blissercize
Purpose: Remove confusion and bring what you enjoy to the surface

Continue your Now or Breath Exercise from the previous lessons. These new exercises will allow you to start bringing to the surface what is already there. It will also prepare you for the next lesson. Take off your thinking hat and don't judge what you write down... just write until you exhaust all your thoughts.

1. Write down what you **don't** enjoy doing. Sometimes simply asking ourselves what we *don't* want to do can help us to narrow down the possibilities. Super-wealthy Steve Jobs once said,

"For the past 33 years, I have looked in the mirror every morning and asked myself: 'If today were the last day of my life, would I want to do what I am about to do today?' And whenever the answer has been 'No' for too many days in a row, I know I need to change something."

2. What are your skills? Many people don't realize the usefulness and need for their skills. What are you good at? What would others say you are good at doing? What about the seemingly mundane things (sewing, reading, good driver, sports, etc.). Write these down. For instance, do you like to shop? Did you know there are companies that pay people to shop in stores so they can get feedback on the experience, product, positioning and ease of purchase?

3. What did you enjoy doing as a child? What about now? What would you feel regret for at the end of your life if you didn't do it? What activities or pursuits can you get completely lost in doing? What stirs up your passion? Do you feel like something is beckoning you? *What is it?*

4. What amount of money do you need to fulfill your dream lifestyle? This will require you to do some digging. Many people have no idea how much money they really need. So write down some brief dream lifestyle desires and then get on the Internet and find out how much that would cost you per month. How much would a personal chef cost? How much would it really cost to do 3 mission trips per year? How much does it cost to live in that part of the country or drive that particular car?

Reverse engineer this. Once you know how much money it costs per month for whatever it is you want, divide it by 20 to discover how much you need to make in 20 days a month (5-day work weeks). This is your target goal.

For example, let's say your dream is to do three mission trips a year—one to a Native American reservation, one to India and one to Jamaica. You want to live in New York City, and you want to dance professionally but you know that you need the best dance teacher in New York. How much will it cost for each trip? Find out. How much money will you need to live in New York City based on what the apartments cost there? What are food costs? What about a car? Will you ride the subway? How much will those lessons cost?

To live whatever lifestyle your dream requires, stop long enough to figure it out. It may not unfold exactly like this because acquiring what you need may come through a variety of ways, but it helps you to think clearly through it. You may discover that you need about $120,000 a year to fulfill your dream. How much is that per month? It's $10,000. If you divide that by 20 (5 days per week x 4 weeks), then your financial goal to achieve your dream would be $500 per day, 5 days a week. Now you have a goal based in reality. In fact, once you know how much it would cost, I strongly suggest creating a "cash machine", a small business that will support your dream by creating cash flow. Contact us for resources on how to do that.

5. In what way(s) would you like to make the world a better place (if money were no object)? Even if you think that desire might change in the future, or it seems too big to accomplish, write it down. Remember this is not what you think *others* think you should do. It is what *you* sincerely wish you could do to help make the world better. Think in terms of simple contributions to the world that would make a difference and that would fulfill what's in your heart.

Most likely this exercise has brought to the surface many possibilities about your future. Are there some you should explore? Which ones?

At this point many people say, *"I know what I want to do, but I just don't have the money to do it."* That, my friends, is an illegal statement. First, identify what you want and THEN following the principles in this book, you will learn that money and opportunities will eventually come to support your vision AFTER you have a heart-believable vision and momentum through action.

A Word of Wisdom About Wealth:

One of the places that Christians tend to get hung up is about money. This is especially true since the reaction to abuses of money in the church have caused other Christians to do a pendulum swing all the way to the other side to despising wealth. It is extremely important for you to confront all limiting beliefs that you have about money that may be unscriptural or lack common sense. Remember, your beliefs are building the house of your life. If you are struggling with finances it could be because there are beliefs that are holding you back. If so, you may want to use the following exercise to deal with them:

1. Do You Believe That Money Is Hard to Obtain?

There can be a belief that says money is in short supply, i.e. there isn't enough. Or one can have a belief that making money is hard and difficult, therefore, you either work really, really hard or give up because it is too hard and settle for less. Love thinks outside of the box!

Biblical belief: You can believe and experience that "money comes to me easily and frequently." There is no shortage of money in the world. Creativity is powerful!

Prayer: "Teach me the skills to make money easily."

2. Do You Believe That You Have to Work an Hourly Job to Earn Money?

There are many people in the world that don't work an hourly job and still make lots of money? It can be from an inheritance, or from starting a business that creates a financial flow that allows them to do what they want. Of course, work that job until you can transition into something else, or until you can add another stream of income. But this limiting belief of an hourly wage can set you on a path where you'll never really be able to enjoy the life God gives you. If you had one million dollars invested at 10% interest, you could live off the interest of $100,000 a year without working at all! Make a million and get on with life.

Biblical belief: You can believe that money comes to you from many streams beyond a 9-5 job. Work smart not just hard. Jesus taught an investment mentality with the parable of the talents.

Prayer: "Teach me how to start or buy businesses that will fund my dream."

3. Do You Believe That Money Is the Root of All Evil?

The Bible doesn't say that. It says that the *love* of money is the root of all kinds of evil (1 Tim. 6:10). In other words, we are to *love people* and *use money*, not love money and use people. We are to trust God and not money, but that doesn't mean we aren't supposed to have money.

Biblical belief: Having and using money is not the same as loving and trusting in it.

Prayer: "I trust You to lead me to resources so I can learn to use money, not trust it."

4. Do You Believe That Only Dishonest People Get Rich?

Is that really true? Is it 100% true? When you believe that, the result is you will feel the need to be dishonest to have wealth. So either you will be dishonest or you will give up getting wealth to avoid violating your conscience.

Biblical belief: I will not judge the hearts of others. Abraham and Solomon were wealthy by the blessing of God and wisdom, therefore, my wealth doesn't have to come from dishonesty. Wealth is not just money, it is abundance!

Prayer: "Teach me to see follow wisdom for wealth."

5. Do You Believe That Having an Abundance of Prosperity Should Be Normal For You? Why or Why Not?

Biblical belief: "whatsoever things you ask, believing you shall receive them."

Prayer: "Remind me that there is an abundance for every good work."

6. Why Do You Think Jesus said, *"The poor you will have with you always."*?

Studies of the poor who win the lottery reveal that most of them lose it all and are in debt in less than 3 years. So don't jokingly suggest that the poor are poor because they don't have money.

*Biblical belief: John blessed us saying, **"may you prosper and be in health even as your soul prospers"**.*

Prayer: "If staying in poverty could sometimes be because of a poverty perspective from my soul, then help me see things differently."

7. Do you Believe Money Is Scarce?

Biblical belief: The world is filled with abundance.

Prayer: "Help me see abundance instead of lack."

8. Do You Believe "I Don't Know How to Make Money"?

Biblical belief: "__I can do all things through Christ who strengthens me.__" I can learn to make more money using the skills and passions that I have now. I can learn to invest and multiply my money. Producing wealth is a skill.

Prayer: "I ask for wisdom and know that you God give it liberally. I want to learn."

9. Do You Believe It Is Selfish to Want More Money?

Biblical belief: Actually it is more selfish to want to just get by because just getting by means it is only about you. The more you have, the more you can give to important causes that impact others' lives. You can share more with your wife, your children, your grandchildren and create a legacy for future generations.

Prayer: "Father, I want abundance so I can share it with others."

10. Do You Believe Money Is Not Really That Important?

Tell your mortgage company, utility company and car loan company that money isn't important and see what they think. They will smile as they repossess your car and foreclose on your house.

Biblical belief: _If money wasn't important, then why did Paul say that God would supply all our needs according to His riches in glory in Christ Jesus? Why did Paul receive offerings? Why was he a tent-maker? He did it so that he could travel and share the gospel. He did it so he could help others. Money is important as a tool._

Prayer: "Father, I want to make money a friend, not a god. You have given me the dunamis-power to get wealth. Show me how."

If you feel you have some limiting beliefs about wealth, use this exercise now:

The Wealth Exercise:

1. Take a moment and be thankful for love. Drink it in for a few minutes.

2. Now take out your journal again and ask yourself these questions:

> A. Can I know with 100% absolute certainty that this negative/limiting belief I have is true?
>
> Why might it not be true? Write down any and everything that comes to mind.
>
> B. Is it at all possible that there are other scriptures or understandings of God that I have not considered or been made aware of? Is it possible that God may want to change this belief? Yes or no?

3. Next, write down the opposite of that negative belief. For

example, if it is "I don't know how to make money," write the opposite, "I am learning skills to build wealth!"

4. Once you write that positively, do a "heart-belief buster". This means use your journal to write down in short ideas and statements any thoughts that come to you when you say that statement positively. It may take 10 minutes to allow all the thoughts, positive and negative to come out of the darkness of your heart into the light. Don't judge them, just write… and your perspective will softly change.

Let's say you wrote, "I am learning skills to build wealth!" You might write down, "We grew up poor and I never understood anything else." "My parents always said money doesn't grow on trees." "I have learned other skills in my life." "Maybe I can learn to build wealth." "But I don't know any wealthy people." "Of course, I could pray and ask for wealthy instructors in my life, or to be pointed to books that would help." Once you have exhausted any and all thoughts, you are done. By itself, simply bringing them to the light will often dispel the negative beliefs.

5. What would my life look like if this positive belief was true? Write it down.

6. Prayer: "Father I want to acknowledge every good thing that is in me by Christ Jesus and every good thing about You. Since I need this new belief established in my heart, supply faith to me with evidences, encouragement and signs that it is true."

7. Now sit in His presence in the present with any residual negative emotions and just let them pass through you. Ask God to cleanse your heart with His life, love and light. Rest in that moment like you are simply watching it happen until you sense release and peace.

What Do YOU Want? Accepting Your Desires

"I can teach anybody how to get what they want out of life. The problem is that I can't find anybody who can tell me what they want."
-Mark Twain

I was stunned by how true Mark Twain's statement was when I heard it. Over the last twenty years I've watched so many who are stuck in life because even though they want life to be better than it already is, they can't describe a vision of their future. Or serving a company's vision for so long has stolen their ability to accept that their desires are important. Years of discouragement, of following everyone else's plans, or of bad teaching cover up what they really want.

Then it happened to me, and after a painful transition in ministry, I had to start this process for myself. It took me a couple of years to shift into what I wanted to do with the next 20 years of my life. I had to confront my own limiting beliefs and come to terms with what I really wanted.

I had to learn that I am not my business and my identity is not "pastor". I spent years of my life where everything about my relationship with God was tied to "church". Everything we prayed about, everyone we prayed for, seeking vision for ministry... everything. We lived and breathed that world. So when we shifted out of that role, I realized how much my identity was tied to that position.

I needed to get free of the false idea that being a "pastor" was my life. My life is my spirit and heart within me. My life is expressed in my relationships with my family. Church was just an expression of it, and the success or failure of an organization says absolutely nothing about my value. Jesus was a son before He did any ministry.

It was quite a struggle to separate what I really wanted to do with my life when I was trained that it was inseparable from a religious organization. As those desires emerged, and as I began to value them, amazing things began to happen. Doors opened, life shifted, dreams I didn't know were there started to emerge. I am excited to tell you that I'm watching them come to pass!

One of the reasons I wrote this book is to give you the tools I have been re-using in my own life. They are powerful and effective!

What do YOU Want?

Desire is not sinful. Your desires are God-given. A desire for food, for sex, for rest and for success came from God. Are there boundaries for those desires so that they don't harm us or others? Absolutely. Yet, by being overly focused on overcoming "inordinate" desires and trying to crush them, you may have embraced the idea that all desire is bad. Not so. In fact, God *gives us* the desires of our heart. Tapping into that stream of desire is a healthy way for you to discover the real YOU created in Christ. What do *YOU* want?

Someone will say, *"I'm supposed to be content, aren't I?"* Yes, but not with the definition you are currently using. Contentment is living in the present moment and finding happiness inside of yourself, instead of in things or destinations. It literally means *self-sufficiency. Helps Greek Word Dictionary* defines it as, "properly, self-sufficient, content in the sense of being satisfied because of living in God's contentment (fullness)."

It is vital to be content, to start living from spiritual happiness. This is what is called true faith. True faith is resting in the joy of who God is to us right now. This kind of spiritual happiness is the only way to truly be able to pursue a dream. Otherwise, you will think that you can't be happy until you achieve some purpose or reach some goal. But that isn't true.

I like what actor Jim Carrey said, *"I think everybody should get rich and famous and do everything they ever dreamed of so they can see that it's not the answer."* Contentment is in finding peace and joy NOW from your knowledge of God's love for you. The fulfillment of goals is icing on the cake.

Jesus said, ***"Whoever drinks of ME will never thirst again."*** Thirst was a sign of a curse in the Old Covenant. You, on the other hand, have a fountain of water springing up within you right now. Nothing is more life-giving than the knowledge that God is absolutely, perfectly in love with you. And this is what keeps one happy, satisfied and provides a never-ending fountain of life-giving love. In contentment with God, we are compelled to share that love with others *through* our unique design. In this way, you become a shooting star, not a falling star!

Before we go any further, begin to thank God for His perfect love for you. Thank Him that He loves you even in your failures. He loves you just the way you are, even though He is maturing you. He loves you; not your version of you, but the *truth* about you, and it doesn't make Him want to abandon you. Thank Him that He calls you righteous, forgiven, accepted, powerful, etc. Drink in that truth for a few moments.

Blaze a Trail:

I believe that everyone is born a pioneer. Every baby, without any instruction, without any developed language skills, is—from conception—growing, maturing, and learning. That baby wants to understand and experience life. It is built into us. You are a pioneer too, even if teachers or parents tried to limit you. We can't blame them. Someone limited them at some point as well.

Two roads diverge in a wood and I took the one less traveled. Good advice? It depends. At this point, it is important for me to say that there's nothing wrong with following proven models or imitating the methods of others who are successful. Many times the wheel doesn't need to be reinvented. But the direction of your life ultimately should not be directed by outside voices. God gives us the desires of our heart because He is the One who put them there to begin with.

"Your time is limited so don't waste it living someone else's life. Don't be trapped by dogma, which is living with the results of others people's thinking. Don't let the noise of others' opinions drown out your own inner voice. And most importantly, have the courage to follow your heart and intuition. They somehow already know what you truly want to become. Everything else is secondary." - Apple Founder, Steve Jobs

God's truth is universal and not contained in a denomination or a building. Those who have lived their dreams are operating on God's principles whether they know it or not. That is one of the ways we can know that it's true... because it works for everyone!

The Authenticity Test:

What about those people who genuinely dreamed of becoming famous on American Idol, yet their auditions reveal they had no natural ability to sing? Well, they got some of their hearts desire. Millions of people heard them sing on television, but it wasn't exactly what they had in mind. Some of you may be afraid of that kind of self-deception. That kind of confusion can easily be lifted by the simplicity of listening to the kindness and wisdom of outside voices who have our very best in mind.

That confused person has yet to discover the grandeur of what is really within and is trying to fulfill someone else's dreams for them. I've met people like that before. They are convinced that they can sing like a songbird because a parent or friend, fearful of hurting them, told them they could do anything. I have also seen them doggedly determined to share their "gift" with the world even when they are told the truth. Sadly they were missing what they were truly created for lying right under the surface of their own hearts. This is not authenticity.

I have always wanted to help and teach others. The expression of that has taken several forms. I once had a martial arts school. I was preparing to move to Colorado Springs, CO to hopefully train with the US Olympic training team when I felt I should go into full-time ministry instead. The specifics changed, but the desire to excel and help others to do the same never changed.

After 20 years of pastoral ministry, I am now investing my time in traveling, writing books, and creating materials to mentor others. I am committed to teaching life-giving truths which others are often afraid to share. Though I desire a number of things, helping others through teaching is a core design of my life. What is *yours*?

Blazing a trail is taking the path of your authenticity no matter what people think because you are being motivated by the love of Christ. Paul said, *"The love of Christ compels me"*.

Your Path May Be Polarizing:

One time I loaded up about 6 hours of positive, inspiring meditations on my iPhone and put my head-phones in and went to sleep at night. My experiment was to see if they had any influence on my heart when I woke up. Instead, several times I would wake up around 5 A.M. in the middle of a bad dream of me being arrested, or going to jail. Obviously this wasn't working because it was the opposite of the meditations.

Then one morning I woke up after a seemingly odd dream. This time I decided to see if maybe God or my heart was trying to tell me something. I dreamed that I put a beautiful but dangerous Bengal tiger in a fence and then covered it up with a tarp to hide it. Apparently I didn't want it to get out or for anyone to see it. Then there was water everywhere so I climbed up a ladder to turn off the power because I didn't want anyone to get shocked.

After considering the dream for a few minutes I realized what it meant. The "real" me was the tiger, beautiful and powerful. But I wanted to cover it up and keep it within man-made boundaries because I was afraid of what might happen. In fact, I thought people might be "shocked" at who I really was, so I turned off the power.

One of the hurdles over which most of us need to jump is our need to please everyone else. People want to conform you to their image of who you should be.

Jesus, the manifestation of the love of God, said, *"I did not come to bring peace, but a sword."* Wow. I thought He was the

Prince of peace? Yes, He is. The angels said that He was bringing *"peace on earth, good will toward men."* What He meant by that bit of hyperbole was that as He walked His path in relationship with His father, He refused to be diverted. As He said to John the Baptist, *"blessed is he who is not offended because of Me."* Isn't it amazing that perfect unconditional love from the Son of God himself was polarizing? Love, grace, kindness, mercy and forgiveness only brought division to the hearts which were offended by the goodness of God. Why do we expect it to be different for us?

By its very nature, your journey will polarize people. It will happen. Haters are gonna hate! Get over it. Go ahead and be the loving version of *you* that God created and if people are repelled because of where they are in their life, then they weren't ever going to be a part of your future journey, anyway. Don't carry them with you in your head. Just remember, though, you will begin to attract like-minded people who will support the very things that others reject.

Paul said, *"As much as it is within you, be at peace with all men."* That doesn't mean that at the cost of your destiny you should become a people-pleaser. Only the authentic version of you is going to be fully engaged and happy. Being less than your loving, vibrant, purposeful self is a violation of your very design. You will never be truly happy unless you are authentic! It means be at peace with others even if they won't be at peace with you.

Tear down the fence and let the tiger out!

We had a sign over the entrance into the sanctuary at a church we pastored that said this, *"Be aware, today you may be the answer to another person's prayer."* Loving your dream and seeing it come true will touch many lives. Some will be changed, encouraged, provided for and blessed because of you. So don't hold back. Reject rejection and focus on the many who have been praying for you to bring them the answer to their need.

There is a line in one of my all-time favorite Disney movies called _Tomorrowland_ where a young boy comes to the World's Fair to enter his invention of a jet pack into a contest. A young girl standing by named Athena, said…

Athena: Did you make this yourself?
Young Frank Walker: Yeah.
Athena: Why?
Young Frank Walker: I guess I got tired of waiting around for someone else to do it for me?

Learn from others, but don't wait to follow others. Take your own path!

The Motivation Exercise:

What is the motivation underneath it all? Maybe that person who can't sing is really motivated by being on stage and actually has a career in acting. Dig just a bit deeper than "I love to sing"… rather, what is it that you love *about* singing? Is it moving people to tears or inspiring others from the stage?

What feels true to you? Be totally honest with yourself. If it really isn't your motivation to "do ministry" then don't say that it is because it is "expected" of you. If you feel deeply motivated to make money, it doesn't mean you are greedy. This is about tapping into hidden motivations of love that are unique to you.

☐ I am motivated by the love of helping people.
☐ I am motivated by the love of being successful in all areas

of life.

- ☐ I am motivated by the love of making people smile and laugh.
- ☐ I am motivated by the love of helping people to shake off limitations and walk into their good future.
- ☐ I am motivated by the love of pioneering basics and foundational truths in people's lives.
- ☐ I am motivated by the love of seeing things in others that they can't see in themselves.
- ☐ I am motivated by the love of teaching others.
- ☐ I am motivated by the love of making money for the comfort of my family and for the blessing of others.
- ☐ I am motivated by the love of challenges that are given to me to overcome.
- ☐ I am motivated by the love of projects for which I am able to organize and create details.
- ☐ I am motivated by the love of helping sick people become healthy, or to help poor people become wealthy, or to help struggling couples to find unity.
- ☐ I am motivated to introduce people to Jesus and/or spiritual growth.
- ☐ I am motivated to
- ☐ I am motivated to
- ☐ I am motivated to

Heart Truth 7—The Heart Is the Place of Intentions

The intentions of your heart are not about will power. It is the choice of the heart at rest to actively turn its attention to something. Why do you get focused on something? Because you intended it.

Goethe said, *"Concerning all acts of initiative and creation, there is one elementary truth, the ignorance of which kills countless ideas and splendid plans; that the moment one definitely commits oneself, then Providence moves too. All sorts of things occur to help one that would never otherwise have occurred. A whole stream of events issue from the decision, raising in one's favor, all manner of unforeseen incidents and meetings and material assistance which no man could have dreamed would have come his way. Whatever you can do or dream you can, begin it. Boldness has genius, power and magic in it. Begin it now."*

Napoleon Hill in his classic book, *Think and Grow Rich*, told the story about a pastor named Dr. Frank Gunsaulus who wanted to start a new kind of school after realizing that the traditional teaching methods were inadequate. He needed one million dollars to start the school, but he was making no progress until one day he made an intention in his heart. He determined that he was going to have the money that he needed and that he would have it within a week. He soon had an idea, so He contacted the local newspaper and had them print the title to his upcoming sermon: "What I Would Do if I Had a Million Dollars."

That Sunday Dr. Gunsaulus prepared as if he was already in possession of his answer. Then he preached his message on Sunday morning without his notes with all of his heart. At the end of the message a guest in the service stood up and slowly made his way down the aisle. He said, "Reverend, I liked your sermon. I believed you would do everything you said you would if you had a million dollars. To prove that, I believe in you and your sermon; if you will come to my office tomorrow morning, I will give you the million dollars! My name is Philip D. Armour."

This pastor received the money that he needed for his dream from the famous industrialist of his day within 36 hours of making an intention in his heart! What are the intentions of your heart? Are you just wishing?

In Joe Dispenza's book *Breaking the Habit of Being Yourself: How to Lose Your Mind and Create a New One,* he revealed the results of a study that found when a person held a test tube with strands of DNA in deionized water and then created positive feelings of love along with an intention of the heart to unwind the DNA samples, some were unwound as much as 25 percent! That is the *dunamis*-power of love in action!

So as you approach your destiny without engaging the intentions of your heart, without purposing in your heart to trust, then there is an incongruity and a dissonance in the heart. But when we put those together—the *emotion* and the *intentions* and the *images* of the heart—we just activated the most powerful tool that we never knew we had.

When you feel in your heart the motivation of love behind your dreams and tap into your own authentic dream and intend for it to be fulfilled, you are setting a miracle in motion. Suddenly doors magically open, opportunities arise, people suddenly begin to favor you, situations shift for your good, energy emerges, skills develop quickly and momentum begins.

You can "try" something, and since that is the intention of your heart, the only strength that comes to back it up is the strength for you to "try". As soon as you have tried a bit, you will be done with it. Too many just "try" out jobs, life or marriages, and wonder why they don't work out. It is simple. Often their intention was half-hearted.

On the other hand, if you intend to finish, do you know what will happen? You will finish. If you intend to make money, it will happen. When you intend to succeed, your life will become unstoppable. For years I wished I could go on a mission trip but the money was never there. One day I made a choice in my heart that I was going to go. I didn't know how I could afford it but I was going. You know what happened don't you? Every penny I needed came to me in a very short period of time.

If you intend to discover the next steps for your life, you will find them.

If you intend to act on those, then there is grace that comes to back you up and fulfill the dreams in your heart.

What do YOU WANT? What do YOU intend to happen for your life?

Exercise: Crack Your Heart DNA Code

In 1953, James Watson and Francis Crick revealed the structure and properties of DNA, the molecule that carries our genetic information. What they discovered was that the blueprint for a human being was encapsulated in a long string of nucleic acid arranged in a double helix, like a twisted rope ladder with three billion rungs. For this discovery, Watson and Crick, together with Maurice Wilkins, were awarded a Nobel Prize in 1962.

Your spirit coded your heart with unique destiny DNA. Would you like to crack the code of your Heart DNA? Here is one of the ways to begin. Remember 1 Samuel 9:19, *"Samuel answered Saul and said, "I am the seer. Go up before me to the high place, for you shall eat with me today; and tomorrow I will let you go and will tell you all that is in your heart."*

Start by praying, *"Father guide my heart."* Take a moment for a breath prayer.

I learned this method from Lance Wallnau and it's a powerful way to excavate what is already in your heart.

1. Write down the top ten Dream Points for your ideal life. This is not about exaggerated, grandiose things that really aren't in your heart. Instead, write down the top ten things you want to do in order to have no regrets. This is not the *how to*, but the *what*. Brainstorm...dump everything you can onto a piece of paper and then identify the top ten. "I would love it if I looked back on my life and did these things and fulfilled these dreams..." It is about the *desires of your heart*!

2. Take these 10 and put them in order of importance. If you could only fulfill one of these, and were forced to give up the rest, which one would you choose? Don't compromise here. Number 1 must be the MOST important. Then with the others on the list ask the same question. If I could only do one of these which would it be? Number 4 must be more important to you than number 5. And so on. This is not in order of others' expectations. These are about *your* dreams and passions and the importance they have in *your* heart. What do you FEEL they are instead of what you THINK they ought to be?

3. Can any of these be combined? Could you accomplish some of these together? Do some of them overlap? If so, join them together and then go through your importance exercise again. Do this until it is clear what your top three are.

4. Now say it out loud to yourself as if it were real NOW, and as statements of love. This is where you speak as if it were present tense and already true. Speak from your inner-most being, as the true you filled with life, accepted by God, full of destiny! Voicing it empowers it.

For example: I am designed by God to be a spiritual mentor! I enjoy living in Nashville, TN but also love vacationing in the Caribbean twice a year. I lead mission trips to poverty-stricken areas of the world and love teaching them the good news and practical ways of living. I love netting $20,000 a month from consulting, coaching, providing resources and in my businesses which are funding my dream. I love being free from a 9-5 job and using my spare time to learn to dance, to sing and connect deeply with others.

Say your dream out loud frequently! Say it literally looking in a mirror. Do it now, with intention! Then write your declaration down in your journal.

5. Maybe you feel some inner resistance to your goal or dream? This next exercise can be eye-opening because it starts to bring to the surface some of the limiting beliefs that could hold you back. As simple as it appears, it is a very powerful tool to move you forward!

DON'T SKIP THIS. Honesty with your heart is the key here.

Write down as many answers to these two questions that you can possibly imagine, no matter how crazy it sounds.

A. What is keeping you from having this dream/desire fulfilled now?

B. What could you do to get this dream/desire fulfilled?

Once you are done exhausting everything you can imagine, you have created for yourself two lists. The first one demonstrates what you *think* are limitations. The second one *demonstrates* the possibilities.

Jesus said, *"**All things are possible to him that believes**"*, yet we tend to focus only on the *possible* part. We don't realize ALL the different possibilities of HOW and so our vision and faith are locked in our limited perspective. When you dream of the multiple possibilities of HOW, *then* your heart begins to see how easy the possibilities are to overcome those obstacles. Put on your creativity hat and give it a try. Get someone to brainstorm with you. Be silly and creative with it.

For each of the reasons that seemed to have an emotional punch for why it wasn't happening right now in your life, use the exercise below for each reason/belief.

1. Take a moment and be thankful for love. Drink it in for a few minutes.

2. Now take out your journal again and ask yourself these questions:

> A. Can I know with 100% absolute certainty that this negative/limiting belief I have is true? Are these things really holding me back?

> Why might it not be true? Write down any and everything that comes to mind.

> B. Is it at all possible that there are other scriptures or understandings of God that I have not considered or been made aware of? Is it possible that God may want to

change this belief? Yes or no?

3. Next, write down the opposite of that negative belief. What would the positive life-giving belief be?

4. Once you write that positively do a "heart-belief buster". This means use your journal to write down in short ideas and statements any thoughts that come to you when you say that statement positively. It may take 10 minutes to allow all the thoughts, positive and negative, to come out of the darkness of your heart into the light. Don't judge them, just write… and your perspective will softly change.

By itself, simply bringing them to the light will often dispel the negative beliefs.

5. What would my life look like if this positive belief was true? Write it down.

6. Prayer: "Father I want to acknowledge every good thing that is in me by Christ Jesus and every good thing about You. Since I need this new belief established in my heart, supply faith to me with evidences, encouragement and signs that it is true."

7. Now sit in His presence in the present with any residual negative emotions and just let them pass through you. Ask God to cleanse your heart with His life, love and light. Rest in that moment like you are simply watching it happen until you sense release and peace.

PART 4

STEP INTO YOUR FUTURE NOW!
Manifesting the Miracle

The Extraordinary World of Abundance: Love What You Want

"Clarity of mind means clarity of passion, too; this is why a great and clear mind loves ardently and sees distinctly what it loves."
–Blaise Pascal, Mathematician and Philosopher

In the early 1970's, discovering diseases like cancer at an early stage was very difficult. Dr. Raymond Damadian, the "father of the MRI", was doing experiments with nuclear magnetic resonance to differentiate certain bacteria. Soon he realized the technology could be used on the human body to detect diseases with a high degree of accuracy. Now millions of scans are done each year that save lives.

All the elements of an MRI machine existed from the moment of creation. It wasn't until our lifetime, though, that the knowledge and know-how existed. He didn't create it from nothing. The possibility of its existence was always here, but our awareness of it eventually expanded to enable us to do things that were seemingly impossible before.

Everything you need already exists. That means there is no such thing as lack. Lack is a mindset, a poverty heart belief and an illusion which is fostered by television, politicians, and bad theology. For dreams to come true we need to expand our heart awareness to see a universe filled with abundance.

James said, *"Every good and perfect (mature, full grown) gift (is coming) down from the Father of lights with whom there is no variation nor shadow of turning."* (James 1:17)

There is an unending supply of God's intrinsic goodness coming to us as gifts of grace from which God is unrelenting and unyieldingly determined for us to experience. Close your eyes for a moment and just imagine the multitude of gifts that are racing toward you from every direction. There are, right now, a limitless amount of possibilities, opportunities and ways to answer your every need. You are a part of a *yes and amen* Gospel in which all the promises are yes and amen in Christ Jesus. He says yes! His supply is constant! He is unrelenting and unyielding in providing!

The only lack is our own awareness. Once you start to believe in an abundant universe you will start to look at the glass, not as half empty, nor even as half full. You will see it full of water and air...completely *full*! Sometimes we are like the elder brother in the story of the prodigal son; we live in the Father's house of abundance, everything He has is ours, but we experience the limitations of the imaginary house that our beliefs have built.

"You are blessed with every spiritual blessing in the heavenly places in Christ Jesus" (Ephesians 1:3). Because Christ is the Blessed One and you are in Christ, then every empowering blessing and favor is already yours. You can't get any more favor than you have right now. We, like Christ in His earthly ministry, can grow up into the favor we already possess. In fact, the whole universe is chocked full of God's glorious, good *yes and amen* presence. Ephesians 4:6, ***"... one God and Father of all, who is over all, and through all, and in all."***

Ephesians 4:10, ***"And the same One who descended is the One who ascended higher than all the heavens so that He might fill the entire universe with Himself"*** (NLT). There is no place God is not. All creation is within him. Imagine if you will, a giant bowl of water. Inside that bowl of water are marbles and sponges. God is both the bowl and the water, and everything in creation is saturated and within Him. All that God is, is in all places at the same time. Abundance should be the vision of our hearts all the time. The very instant of asking in Singapore creates an instantaneous answer in New York because God is above all, through all and in all!

God's Love for All:

John 3:16, one of our favorite Sunday School verses says, *"For God so loved the world that He gave His only begotten Son that whosoever believes in Him will not perish but have eternal life."* Of course we apply that to everybody in the world, right? Yes, that is true. But do you know what the word "world" is? It is the word ***kosmos*** and means the whole created universe including people. For God so loved the entire created order, the sun, the moon, the stars, the trees, the atoms, the quantum level of material, the mountains, the planets, the air, the flowers. He loves absolutely everything that He created. He is in love with life in every dimension! Are you?

Did you know that Paul said in 1Timothy 6:17 that God ***"...richly supplies us with ALL things to enjoy"*** (NAS)?

Paul goes on to say, *"So then let no one boast in men. For all things belong to you, whether Paul or Apollos or Cephas or the world or life or death or things present or things to come; ALL things belong to you..."* (1 Corinthians 3:21-22) All things are yours? Yes. That is exactly what he said!

Jesus, said, *"how much more will your heavenly Father give good things to those who ask."* (Matthew 7:11)

We can trust that every good thing that we want is ours. Everything that we want to enjoy *can* be ours to enjoy. So why then are we not enjoying life? Because we, like God, are called to love life and all that is in it. See, *faith* works through *love*. If we don't love the good things God has for us, then how can we have confidence in our hearts that our dreams will come true?

It is okay for you to love 1966 Ford Mustang GT's with blue and white stripes and deluxe pony interior with an automatic transmission and console. Yes, that is my love. It is okay for you to love movies and skydiving and Star Wars. It is okay for you to love sex with your spouse. You are encouraged to enjoy food and maybe even a glass of wine at the wedding at Cana where Jesus made hundreds of gallons for the party.

When John said, **"Do not love the world or the things of this world"** he explains what he means: **"the lust of the flesh, the lust of the eyes and the pride of life"** (1 John 2:15-16).

"Worldliness" isn't a synonym for loving and enjoying life. Some actually teach that having pleasure in life is anti-christian hedonism. Those are the ones who walk around looking like they suck the souls of lemons for breakfast. In fact, the one who struggles with worldliness according to John *doesn't have the love of the Father in them.* It doesn't say they don't love the Father; it says that they don't have within themselves a *revelation* of the Father's agape, unconditional, all inclusive, God-kind of love. When you know God will richly supply you with good things to enjoy, you don't have to covet after them in the wrong ways. God will give you the good to enjoy because He loves you too.

Remember, the entire universe was created in harmony with love so abundance *is* the gift from His love. **If you love it, there's plenty of it!** Knowing that, is it any wonder that He makes such broad statements as, *"Ask and you shall receive"*?

See, we further limit ourselves by saying *"I'm not sure if providing this or giving me that is the will of God"* when He says the will of God is *"**Whatsoever** things you ask, believing that you receive them, you shall have them."* (Matthew 21:22) The limitations are only those we allowed to be placed on our own hearts. God has left the door wide open. Would *love* give you what you are asking? What we tend to do is bring God's *yes*, His unlimited supply, His promise of unmerited favor, His good gifts, His connection to all creation both visible and invisible, and His unlimited promises down to just "maybe."

When Jesus said that *all things are possible to him that believes*, we are not being invited to imagine that in each situation there is only one possible outcome. We are being challenged to see that there are limitless possibilities in each situation. ALL things are possible means there are *ALL kinds of possibilities in each circumstance. Every good and perfect gift comes down from the Father of lights without variation or shadow of turning*. There is an unending stream of invisible gifts and possibilities waiting for you to choose by asking and believing.

What is your vision? What do you need? If you start with *"I don't have enough money for that"* then you have already started limiting yourself to your own abilities instead of seeing life from the larger perspective of abundance. You may not physically have it in your hands right now, but can your heart see it as real in the invisible spiritual realm, now? It's like the preacher who understood abundance and said to his congregation one time, "I have good news and I have bad news. The good news is that there is more than enough money to build a brand new sanctuary.

The bad news is that it is still in your pockets."

My God shall supply all my need according to His riches (His abundance) in glory in Christ Jesus. Paul said that in the context of his own personal mission. There is a supply for your mission, too.

The Secret of the Abundant Universe!

Philosopher Søren Kierkegaard said, *"When one has once fully entered the realm of love, the world- no matter how imperfect- becomes rich and beautiful- it consists solely of opportunities for love."*

The universe is not only extremely abundant, it is also saturated with love. The most powerful force in the universe isn't a nuclear bomb or even the "all-mightiness" of God. The most powerful force in the universe is love. There is no attribute of God that supersedes His love. Love is not an attribute. It is his nature. God IS love and this love is incredibly and magnificently abundant throughout creation. Every attribute of God flows out of love. It isn't love *and* justice. His justice cannot be separated *from* His love, therefore all His justice is redemptive, not destructive.

By the way, if you struggle with understanding some of the "difficult" passages in the Bible and you want to see them from a fresh, grace-based lens, go to my website and feast on wonderful teaching (www.ANewDayDawning.com).

Love is this reality that humanity was blinded to in the garden. After Adam and Eve covered themselves with fig leaves, the all-knowing God began to "look" for them and call for them while they were hiding. He wasn't stomping through the garden in fury because of their failure. He didn't cease being love to them. But the moment they ate of the tree of religion, they were blinded to the fact that they were created in the image of God and they were blind to the God of the image. They projected their insecurities onto God and became afraid of the god they created in their own hearts.

Jesus came to reveal the Father, and more than anything else to reveal the love of the Father. This is what God is like. Love. The universe was created with love. You were created with love. So nothing in life functions normally or correctly without tapping into love. This is what Jesus came to do. He came to reconnect us to the Source of love through His life, death, burial and resurrection. Nothing is more important than when you experience, accept and begin living from the love of God.

"As He IS, so are we in this world," said the Apostle John. God is LOVE. For your life to make sense, for your inner purpose to awaken and for your life goals to emerge, you MUST begin to embrace love and give it away. We are to BECOME love!

Love is patient, love is kind. But God is love. It means God is patient. God is kind. All of what it means for you to be is summed up as a gift of His love. He created you to be accepted, forgiven, delighted in, righteous, and near Him, all because of love! So let's talk about "what's love got to do with it". Check out what love has to do with *your inner purpose, and your outward goals and purposes.*

In the New Covenant, Jesus turned everything upside down because He was trying to demonstrate that you are not called to be the source. He is. So in the Old it said, *love the Lord your God with all your heart, mind, soul and strength and love your neighbor as yourself.* But in the New Covenant Jesus introduced a new commandment. The word "new" is *kainos* meaning "brand new, as we haven't done it like this before." He says, *"A new commandment I give to you that you love one another AS I have loved you."* He flipped the tables and made Himself the Source of love so that when you receive it first, you have the capacity to give it away to others.

The way of the kingdom is that we become the best receivers of love that we can be, and then we give it away. You cannot give what you don't have, right? Jesus was revealing a powerful truth about life. Instead of demanding love from us, He is instead supplying love to us which He knows will return back to Him. That is why John says, *"not that we loved him, but that he loved us and was the propitiation for our sins..."* It is why John says, *"We love him because he first loved us."* Do you see it?

Jesus was always introducing this new covenant contrast. He said, *"You've heard it said an eye for an eye and a tooth for a tooth, but I say to you, if a person strikes you on the cheek, turn to him the other also."* Why? Because sowing love back into a situation is a powerful force in the universe that doesn't just balance things, it creates new things, it changes things. It is a seed that you give which, even if it is not in that situation, in some way it is coming back to you in your life. You get it from God, you give it away, and then it comes back to you. It is a principle of grace because God gives it to us first.

The Measuring Cup:

Jesus said, *"with the measure that you use, it will be measured back to you."* This is sometimes mistakenly thought to mean that God will measure it back to us. But in the context, He is talking about judging. Don't try this at home, but if you want to start a fight with your spouse or best friend, judge their heart.

Universally, when we judge others (unless they are very mature), it will come back as angry judgment to us. We also end up using the standard of measurement on ourselves. When we judge others and say, "They don't love me", inevitably a belief is measured back to our own heart as "If they don't love me, I may be unlovable."

One of the great lessons of life is that you cannot judge people and love them at the same time! Judgment clouds our vision. So, everything I want in life, I must get with the help of other people. To not love humanity is to cut off our own dreams. **One of the ways to test the authenticity of your dream is to ask yourself if your dream will intersect the lives of other people.** Will your dream end up impacting others for the better? If not, then it may just be a desire on your part to hide from others and that means you still are not seeing the world through the eyes of love.

"Judge not, and you shall not be judged. Condemn not, and you shall not be condemned. Forgive, and you will be forgiven. Give, and it will be given to you: good measure, pressed down, shaken together, and running over shall MEN give into your bosom. For with the same measure that you use, it will be measured back to you." (Luke 6:37-38, KJV)

Again, none of these are about God's response to us. He took the initiative to sow love, forgiveness, kindness and grace into us. These ideas are about how people and life respond to us. It is not talking about giving an offering in church either. It is about what our lives give to others. So if we give judgment, unforgiveness and condemnation, we will start to see that happening in our life, toward us too. Not from God, but from people. That is why it says, *"pressed down, shaken, and overflowing will MEN give into your bosom."*

127

But on the other hand, if we participate in the generosity of God and give good things, like love, truth, and the gift of our dream's and talents, it will come back to us in this life both in the measure we use, and many times overflowing even more. This is the incredible power that you have to shape the experiences of your life. Jesus sowed love and forgiveness into the world at the crucifixion, and the result was that we love Him because He *first* loved us. He knew it would return back to Him pressed down, shaken together and overflowing.

Or as Rhonda Byrne once said, "Life isn't *happening* to you; life is *responding* to you!" God is *happening* to you, but life around us is often *responding* to what you are doing with what God gives you. If you don't believe it, look your spouse in the eyes and say something that totally judges his/her heart. Or say something totally judgmental on Facebook about politics and watch the sparks fly!

Meditate a moment on that statement! **"Life isn't happening to you; life is *responding* to you!"** Start taking responsibility for your life instead of blaming others. God takes the initiative, and because of grace, He gives seed to the sower. He gives you the seed of a dream, the seed of finances, the seed of love, and the seed of grace. Then what you do with it is up to you. That is His grace. He is the primary Source of your miracle.

The kind of life that you have is often determined by what you do with the seed. If you measure it back out in fullness, then a world will arrange itself around you that you previously thought impossible.

Do you want an awesome marriage? Then celebrate the good marriages that you see around you instead of becoming jealous.

Do you want a promotion? Then rejoice and value the person who got the promotion that you didn't get. Each circumstance is nothing more than an opportunity to sow into your destiny by loving your dream even when you see it in others. Their dream fulfilled is an invitation and promise to you, not a message that you can't have it or a provocation to envy.

Love the world by living your dream. Get it?

In Deuteronomy 8:18 it says, *"And you shall remember the LORD your God, for it is He who gives you the power to get wealth..."* While we are not under the Law, by His grace He has given you the power to get wealth. Most of the time you aren't going to wake up and accidentally receive a check from Publishers Clearing House. This power is the *dunamis* power to love through everything that we do so that what we sow in love comes to us in abundance in a thousand different ways. Wealth is not money; it is abundance in every form.

Salesmen have a bad reputation because some were taught to operate outside of love with manipulative sales techniques. But when the customer feels that the salesman loves the product and cares about them so much that he can't imagine them not having it... sales become easy.

Love is the power that changes your life inside and out. Loving life brings life into your day. Loving your dream helps bring your dream into reality. Think of the kind of leverage you have with life; you can learn the same thing Jesus tried to teach us— give love and it will come back to you. The world of abundance and the world of love are connected and when you connect those dots, things start to happen because this is how life works.

Giving in every form is a participation in the nature of God who is generous. If you want life in abundance, but you won't receive love from God and won't love yourself, then how do you think you are going to get a different harvest? You have God's power to get abundance into your life. You can experience abundance and it all begins with learning to receive love and then give it away.

I love mission trips. A few years ago I led a team to another country and the pastors told us, "Many people come here and preach, but no one has *loved* us like this before!" Years later I met a new friend from a different part of of that nation who oversees many churches there. I was prayerfully considering coming to their region. After I shared this, he in turn said, "Six years ago I had a vision of a man from the USA coming to minister to us! I saw you in the vision before I met you!" We sowed love and God gave a vision to a stranger in another part of the country that opened a door six years before we knew it!

Once after sharing the beauty of God's love to a remote area where there had not been a missionary in over 200 years, we were taken to a leper village. The people there were dying, not from leprosy as much as it was from a lack of clean water. The only water available to them was dirty pond water from which they were getting yellow fever and dysentery.

As I held those lepers in my arms, I could not stop the love and compassion from welling up into tears and I made them a promise that we would dig a well for them. I did not have resources, or know how, but because love taps into the abundant universe, within a few months that village had clean water because the *dunamis*-power of love makes a way.

But this isn't just about missions' opportunities. It is about every single thing in life. Is it possible that you are getting in life what you have been sowing in fear, or in love? Is it possible that some of the negative reactions you are getting from others is because they felt negatively judged to begin with? Could it be that everything is falling apart because you see *yourself* as falling apart? Could it be that there isn't an abundance in your life because you grudgingly give to others? Today that can change.

Heart Truth 8—Your Heart Is like a Thermostat... Whatever You Love Will Eventually Become Your Norm.

Did you get that? A thermometer simply measures the temperature in a room. But a thermostat not only measures the temperature, but it regulates the atmosphere by controlling it. Whatever the thermostat is set to, let's say 70 degrees, will be the temperature of the normal environment for that room.

Do you realize that your heart is like that? The beliefs that are embedded there establish the norm for your life. If you get too much beyond those beliefs, your "heart setting" will attempt to sabotage the situation and bring you back to the norm. For instance, if you believe that the world is not full of love and abundance, but that you deserve to be poor because poor is spiritual, then even if you get a great new job, you will feel guilty or nonspiritual. Before long you will probably lose that job.

The only way to change your life is to change the heart beliefs that are regulating it.

Beliefs are also like a tent. When I stretch out that belief to include something new, I will eventually get the experience and environment that comes underneath it.

There is enough! There is enough money circulating through the earth to meet every one of your needs and fulfill every dream. There is more than enough grace to support your destiny. There is more than enough food in the world to feed every person on the planet. There is more than enough "presence" of God that it doesn't run out at the end of a service. You live in a loving and abundant universe! So what is it that you love?

The question then becomes, "How do I change the belief that says the world is not filled with abundance but with lack?"

"Loving the Abundant Life" Exercise
Purpose: to reconnect your heart to the awareness of the abundance universe

THIS MAY BE THE MOST IMPORTANT EXERCISE THAT YOU DO! In this exercise, you are going to discover how to connect your heart awareness to abundance and love.

Step One: Grab your journal each day, preferably first thing in the morning and the last thing at night.

Step Two: Write down everything that you love about your desire from every angle. Feel it. Love it. Afterward, read it or better yet rewrite it each day until your heart connects love and abundance.

The goal here is to connect your heart with love and notice the things that you love and how abundant they are in the world. How is it that you came to fall in love with your spouse? It started with you noticing all the things you enjoyed about him/her. One of the exercises I do with couples who come in for counseling is to have them face each other without saying anything and look into each other's eyes and think of nothing but all the things they love about the other. Inevitably they end up in tears because they reconnect with love instead of getting trapped into seeing what is wrong with them.

So begin by writing down all the things that you love about life, things you love to do, what you love to feel, what sports you love, what you love about your friends, the kind of car that you love, what you love about how God loves you. What is it that you love about God?

Then what is it that you love about your dream/desire? Write it down fully and from every angle. Write how it makes you feel. Let your heart connect.

Step Three: **Give it your all and give it away.**

Remember the movie *Yes Man* where the main character, bank loan officer Carl Allen has become negative, depressed and alienated from life and people? His friends drag him to a motivational seminar and he commits to saying "yes" to everything for a year. Suddenly he is swept into a whirlwind of all kinds of crazy adventures because of his surrender to the power of *yes*.

That is what I am asking you. Not to say yes to everything, but to say YES to love and watch an adventure unfold! There is an energy that comes into your life when you say yes to love that becomes extremely empowering! It won't be in a frenetic psychologically disturbed kind of way. Rather it will feel like energetic peace.

You don't have to love the entire world, just the one in front of you. So I'm encouraging you to go on a love binge. Remember that Jesus gave forgiveness, love, good, and grace even unto death! He held nothing back! Now we love Him because He first loved us. Don't think of this as a passing exercise. Go radical in becoming love to everyone in every situation.

Abandon all your excuses. You will receive back, pressed down, shaken together and overflowing! Saturate your world with love and it will give it back.

Love yourself as a humble gift that the world needs. Love the products that you sell, or the ideas that you possess. Love people for their sake.

Feel like you aren't getting love? Go share it with someone and see what happens. The feeling of love is best felt as it is passing THROUGH you. When you walk by someone on the sidewalk speak a blessing over their life. Pray for those who hurt you. Let good overcome evil. Love your dream. Talk about how much you love your dream to others. It may take a day, a week, or a year. No one knows the exact timing, but what you sow in love will become your reality and you will not only live and love your dream, you will live and love life again!

What You See Is What You Get: The Seeking Factor

"Either you are the creature of circumstances or the creator of your circumstances. You cannot be both."
–Cavett Roberts, co-founder of the National Speakers Association.

What and how we see is everything. I heard a story once about a traveler that came upon an old farmer hoeing in his field beside the road. Deciding to stop and rest, the man got the attention of the farmer and asked a question. "What sort of people live in the next town?" asked the stranger.

The farmer replied with a question: "What were the people like where you've come from?"

"They were terrible, lazy good-for-nothing people. They were the most selfish people in the world and not a one of them to be trusted. I'm so glad to be leaving them behind."

Then the old farmer said, "I'm sorry to hear that. Well, I'm afraid that you'll find the same kind of people in the next town too." Disappointed, the traveler moved along and the farmer returned to his work.

Some time later another stranger, coming from the same direction, got the farmers attention, and they stopped to talk. He, too asked, "What sort of people live in the next town?"

Again the farmer asked, "What were the people like where

you've come from?"

"They were the best people in the world. Hard-working, honest and friendly. I'm sorry to be leaving them."

"Fear not," said the farmer. "You'll find the same sort in the next town."

Do you see? We will always find what we are looking for. Jesus said it like this: Seek and you will find. Whatever you look for, whatever you seek for, you will eventually find. Good or bad. Right or wrong. Dream or nightmare. That means sometimes we need to change *what* we are looking for.

The Washington Post wrote about a cold January morning in 2007 at the DC Metro Station. The man with a violin played six Bach pieces for about 45 minutes. During that time approximately two-thousand people went through the station, most of them on their way to work. After three minutes a middle-aged man noticed there was a musician playing. He slowed his pace and stopped for a few seconds and then hurried to meet his schedule.

4 minutes later: The violinist received his first dollar: a woman threw the money in the hat, and without stopping, continued to walk.

6 minutes later: A young man leaned against the wall to listen to him, then looked at his watch and started to walk again.

10 minutes: A 3-year-old boy stopped, but his mother tugged him along hurriedly. The kid stopped to look at the violinist again, but the mother pushed hard and the child continued to walk, turning his head all the time. This action was repeated by several other children. And every parent, without exception, forced their children to not stop, but to move on quickly.

45 minutes: The musician played continuously. Only 6 people stopped and listened for a short while. About 20 of them gave money, but continued to walk at their normal pace. The man collected a total of just $32.

1 hour: He finished playing and silence took over. No one noticed. No one applauded, nor was there any recognition. No one knew this, but the violinist was Joshua Bell, one of the greatest musicians in the world. He played one of the most intricate pieces ever written, with a violin worth $3.5 million dollars. Two days before, Joshua Bell sold-out a theater in Boston where the seats averaged $100.

This is a true story. Joshua Bell playing incognito in the metro station was planned by *The Washington Post* and Gene Weingarten as part of a social experiment about perception, taste and people's priorities. Some of the questions that were raised were: In a commonplace environment at an inappropriate hour, do we perceive beauty? Do we stop to appreciate it? Do we recognize talent in an unexpected context?

Try this quick exercise. Look around the room and try to remember everything that is red colored or shades of red in the room. STOP now and do it.

Abundance is everywhere. Provision is everywhere. Love is everywhere. The universe is filled with His glory. The question is, do we ever notice? There is an incredible power in simply noticing, but for each of us there is an internal setting that determines *what* we notice. It is what we, ourselves, program into our own hearts.

Now close your eyes and recall everything that was blue instead of red. Difficult, isn't it? Awareness is so powerful. Wherever we turn our awareness is what we will begin to experience.

Heart Truth 9—We Don't See with Our Eyes, We See with Our Hearts.

The brain is a processor of information, but the heart is the place from which we perceive the world. And when painful events happen, our "seer" can get stuck, so focused on pain that we can't see good anywhere, or in anyone, anymore. The way we interpret the world, the way that we perceive whatever is coming into the physical eyes is interpreted by the heart and the images that were already there.

That is why two people at the scene of an accident can see two very different things. It is why a man jumps when he sees a rubber snake. The image he already has of snakes is that they are dangerous, and even though the rubber snake has no power whatsoever to harm, it is interpreted instantly according to the images that are already there. Joshua Bell's music and person were being judged according to preexisting images that a man in the subway playing music is just a common thing, and as a result they could not perceive who he really was.

If we noticed everything about everything we couldn't process it all and we would be totally overwhelmed. So what do we do? Our hearts notice those things that are important to us. We have a preexisting image about where awesome musicians are supposed to play. *In other words, generally speaking, we only see what we already see.* That means we have to make a choice to see anything differently. It means if you want to see something different in your life, you have to begin to seek it first. *Is it possible that you are missing God's gifts of abundance every day? Is it possible that the images that determine who, what, when, where and how are actually blinding you to God's glory everywhere?*

In the book *How to Teach Your Baby Math*, the authors tell of how they came to the amazing conclusion that babies are born geniuses! It began with them working with severely brain damaged babies, in hopes of giving them some kind of minimal normality, but instead they found that these same severely brain damaged babies were able to *read several languages with total understanding, do advanced math, play the violin, do gymnastics, swim, dive, and write computer programs by the age of 4 years old.* Children are born geniuses and an insatiable desire for learning...*BEFORE THEY CAN EVER SAY A WORD!* It means that children are learning from a different form other than lecture. They are learning by sight and by pictures! Children have no language at that age yet they are learning at the speed of sight!

Heart Truth 10—Your Entire Being Is Trying to Fulfill the Images in Your Heart.

Did you know that if you hold a pendulum of any kind, allowing it to dangle straight down and think to yourself over and over again, *"I will not move this pendulum!"*, but then at the same time you use your "image maker" called your heart to imagine it going in circles...do you know what is going to happen? Eventually, it will start moving in circles. Why? Because your whole body is trying to fulfill the images in your heart, not the thoughts in your head! *As a man thinks in his heart, so is he!*

So what happens if your image of yourself is a powerless person? You will keep failing because your entire being is trying to fulfill the vision you believe in your heart! What happens if your image of yourself is a fearful person? If you don't notice who you really are, if you don't have a different image of yourself, then you will keep perceiving the same one and continue to get the same results.

The definition of perception is the ability to see, hear, or become aware of something through the senses. But that is not entirely accurate, because in whatever way the heart "sees" is how your perception is colored. In order to change that, one must change the picture in the heart and then learn to notice something different than they are currently seeing.

Everything in life starts with the invisible and moves to the visible or physical. If you want to have a different life, a life where your dreams are fulfilled, then you will have to see it in your heart differently first. Otherwise, what you will "see" are all the reasons you can't do this, or go there, and you will live accordingly. Or to say it another way, your conscious-thinking-computer-processor-mind is the tip of the iceberg, while your subconscious (heart) is a huge invisible realm from which you *really* make your decisions. All the while we are trying to think new thoughts (which is good), but we make little progress because we miss the point. Our motivations come from deeper within, from the pictures and beliefs of the heart.

God Sees The End From The Beginning. So Should You!!!

Beyond Your Wildest Dreams being fulfilled happens with inward, invisible images. It is found in the wisdom of *"Now to him who is able to do immeasurably more than all we ask or imagine, according to the power that is at work within us..."* (Eph. 3:20, NIV). Beyond what we can imagine assumes we are imagining something for that dunamis power to work through.

That is how God operates and how we partner with God. Many live from the outside-in, and they wonder why things don't work in their lives. When God created Adam and Eve He had an image in His heart from which He created them. They were created in the "likeness and image" of God.

Before the great flood in Genesis it says, *"**The imaginations of their hearts were only evil continually.**"* That which drove their behavior—the images of their hearts——were a continuous stream of evil that the preaching of Noah and the building of the ark did not dislodge. They refused to imagine something different.

According to heart expert Larry Napier, every human being is born with the basic equipment called our "image maker". It is neutral, neither good nor bad. It is what we allow on that screen that determines our experience of life. ***Guard your heart, for out of it flow the issues of life.**** Not only is it true that life is responding TO us, but it is also true that life is happening THROUGH us. Life is experienced through the heart. That is where *dunamis*-power flows through. So this "image maker" we all possess is shaping our lives!

So if God sees the end from the beginning, and then creates based on those pre-imagined ideas, then so should we.

The Process: What You See Is What You Get

Do you realize that God hasn't created anything ex-nihilo (out of nothing) since creation was finished? Not one single thing. If you don't understand this then Beyond Your Wildest Dreams seems impossible and improbable. It will seem like we are trying to get God to create something out of nothing which feels more like we are arm-twisting God for a rare lottery type event.

Let me take you, just for a moment, into how creation came about. We know that Paul says in Colossians 1:16, *"For by Him all things are created that are in heaven and that are on earth, VISIBLE and INVISIBLE..."* So the entire realm of the visible and invisible was created by God. The invisible is a created realm.

In Hebrews 11:3 it says, *"By faith we understand that the worlds were framed by the word of God, so that the things which are seen (visible) were not made of things which are visible."* The world(s), plural, the visible and invisible worlds were created by God, but the visible world was created out of the invisible world He created. Do you see that? Everything visible was created from the material of the invisible world.

In Genesis we see, *"In the beginning God created the heavens and the earth. The earth was without form and void, and darkness was on the face of the deep..."* The words "without form and void" are *tohu* (empty space, formless) and *bohu* (void). God created the invisible massive field of energy then after he created a picture in his heart, an idea in his imagination, he spoke into it, turning what was formless into visible substance.

Everything that is visible was made from or made out of the invisible realm. Let me say it again. What scientists call the quantum world of energy was created first out of nothing, then as God had an image in His heart of what He wanted, He spoke into that invisible world and it took on form in the visible.

So what? We are not God, but could it be that in order for the

142

dream that we love to come to pass, we are to operate in a similar manner? We operate in similar fashion because this is how reality was created. We aren't waiting for God to say yes. He already says *yes and amen* to His promises. We are created in the image of God with *dunamis* power to set miracles in motion.

It means that the world of abundance exists in the form of the potential. What we will see is often what we get.

That is why Andrew Carnegie who was born into poverty and immigrated with his family to the United States from Scotland was able to eventually give away about 350 million dollars during the last 18 years of his life. He discovered the secret to prosperity and explained that, "Any idea that is held in the [heart] that is emphasized, that is either feared or revered, will begin at once to clothe itself in the most convenient and appropriate form available."

Or as Paul said, *"Now to him who is able to do immeasurably more than all we ask or imagine, according to the power that is at work within us…"* (Ephesians 3:20, NIV).

There is a power within you, the *dunamis*-power of love, that is inherent within. There is a power within you—the power to get wealth and access abundance. There is a power within you which is the power to believe and then act on that belief. There is a power within you and it is the power of your imagination. **When these are congruent you begin to see good things miraculously invade your life.**

It is the secret to your destiny. It is the secret of co-creating and co-writing your future with God. Yes, there are things beyond our control that happen TO us, but life can happen THROUGH us when we provide our hearts with an image of the future that we prefer. This, my friends, is so powerful that this is worth many times the price of this book. As we learn to live like this more and more, we will find a realm in which all things really are possible.

Someone might say that what is invisible isn't real. Let me ask you a question please. Can you see love? You can see the effects of love, but love can't be seen with our physical eyes, yet it is real. Wind can't be seen, but it can be felt. What is invisible is real! Imagination doesn't mean imaginary. Imagination is the first step is shaping what will be seen in the physical!

The Television Miracle

In one church that we pastored, I wanted a flat screen TV for the foyer so we could run announcements and enable Moms with crying children to watch and not miss any of the service. I loved the look and practicality of a TV there. Our budget, though, was limited. So for about two weeks, each night before I left the office I would thank God for a flat screen TV and I would imagine myself standing in the foyer looking at it.

Shortly afterward, a woman in the church contacted us and asked if we wanted their 50" flat screen TV which perfectly fit the space in our foyer. Then, a couple of months later, a guy who was new to our church (without any prompting on our part, and without being privy to my desire) asked if we needed any TVs. He had 4 more flat screen TVs that he gave to us. It was more than we needed; abundance above what I asked and imagined.

Hebrews 11:1-2, *"Now faith is the substance of things hoped for, the evidence of things not seen. For by it the elders obtained a good testimony. By faith, we understand that the worlds were framed by the word of God so that the things which are seen were not made of things which are visible."*

So faith isn't an intellectual consent to truths. It is an image and confidence in the place from which we believe—the heart. Therefore, if you want to change what you believe, it isn't about memorizing a bunch of scriptures. David said, *"Thy word have I hidden in my heart"* ...not my head.

Faith is the evidence that we are SEEING-PERCEIVING something with our hearts before we see it in the natural. By faith, we understand that the invisible came first in the creation before the natural. You can't have images in your heart of yourself as a failure and a fool and still expect to have sustainable success and wisdom! On the other hand, if you have images that you love in your heart...well...God will do more than you can imagine.

One of the authors of the *Chicken Soup for the Soul*, Mark Victor Hansen, tells the story that they were turned down over and over again by publishers. So he took Dr. Scott Peck's 12-year *New York Times* list best-seller, *The Road Less Traveled*, as an example. He went to the *Times* and whited out the title and wrote *Chicken Soup for the Soul* in its place as a best-seller. He did that with several newspapers and then cut them out and posted them on walls, in offices, and on mirrors so that they could imagine being a best seller. As you may know, now it is one of the best-selling books of all time, second only to the Bible.

About the time I was learning this my evangelist friend shared his testimony that he would get in his prayer closet and imagine himself healing the sick in downtown Nashville. Shortly after he starting experiencing those same miracles exactly as he was seeing them. So I was preparing for my first trip to India, and for months ahead of time, I would prayerfully imagine myself doing miracles of every kind, and do you know what? *That is exactly what happened!*

You present your heart the images on a consistent basis until it becomes real to your heart, and it will become real in your life. Somehow the *dunamis*-power of love moves *through* the image, and will begin to influence situations and circumstances to give you the desires of your heart!

I'm not talking about magic here. It isn't the image that does anything. The image shapes our believing, and the believing heart is what *dunamis*-power works through. Is it God that flows through that image, or is it the invisible realm God created? Who cares?! I don't need to have an opinion. What I know is that it works for those who know God and those who don't.

The Coincidence Factor

The earliest description of a magnifying glass in 424 BC spoke of how it could be used to take the power of the sun, focus it intensely to start a fire for kindling or to cauterize a wound. It would be used destructively (burn wood), constructively (provide heat) or for healing (of a wound).

Think of your heart as a magnifying glass intensifying the focus of what flows through it, for good or bad. This magnifying glass of the heart is made up of images, intentions, feelings and then "out of the abundance of the heart the mouth speaks." It can make things appear larger than they really are (fear). Or it can be used like a projector to enlarge something good. The miracle comes out from that focus. Focus of attention and focus of heart is powerful.

Commonly, we will begin to see around us what was always there but was hidden because we didn't use our hearts to focus on them. Or to say it another way, we often miss what is right in front of us because we don't notice it. In real estate deals I find that people want to sell their houses with sometimes glaring problems that they no longer notice. Conversely, my wife and I were challenged to find a house to flip in two weeks, and as we started to notice with our hearts, a deal practically fell into our laps within that time.

I also remember hearing once that Native American Indians didn't "see" the Niña, the Pinta or the Santa Maria as they came over the horizon and close to shore. It wasn't because they had a vision problem but because they didn't have a heart-based frame of reference for what a ship looked like.

When our heart's vision gets locked into a perception, it is often difficult to "see" anything else. Not choosing to look for that which is outside our accustomed experience limits our future experiences and keeps us in a loop of seeing and getting the same results out of life.

Once you start the journey of seeing with your heart, you will begin to see "coincidences" that match your seeking. It is like buying a new red sports car and then for the first time noticing red sports cars all over the city. Some things were there all along, while others will be new doors opening right before your eyes. You will find what you are looking for... good or bad. It doesn't mean every coincidence is the right path, but it does mean that they are invitations for you to find out!

Maybe you think that "seeking God" means a prayer meeting or protracted fasting. It doesn't. It just means to "look for Him" and notice around you what He is doing to affirm your new beliefs.

Noticing can be clouded by our persistent judging of everything around us, though. There is probably no better heart habit than being able to look at every situation, every circumstance, each person, even objects around us and notice without judging.

For instance, how much of your heart-energy is taken up as you walk into the kitchen and begin the downward spiral of noticing and judging? You see the dishes that weren't washed from the night before, immediately giving it meaning by judging that:

- "No one ever helps clean the kitchen!"
- "Guests are coming over soon and they will think that I'm a terrible house-keeper."
- "Little Johnny never does his chores. Wait till he gets home! He is in so much trouble!"

Those judgments produce an emotional state that will carry over when your guests arrive and you will fake a happy face, or keep complaining about it to everyone for the rest of the night. How much emotional energy was wasted? By seeing it was more than dishes unwashed on the counter, the entire night could be ruined. Think about it. An inanimate object ruined the night only because you judged the meaning.

All along, there may have been beautiful things you didn't notice:

- A smile on your child's face because he made an A on his test today. He stayed up late studying. That is why he forgot to wash the dishes.
- Your spouse did other chores getting ready for the night which you didn't have to do.

In other words, if our hearts are looking for evidences to reinforce a belief, but then we judge everything as good and bad and constantly give it meaning, we will miss what is important… love. Then we miss our reinforcement of that belief as well.

Jesus said, *"Do not judge according to appearance, but judge the righteous judgment"* (John 7:24, BLB). This cannot mean judge according to a righteous standard of laws and expectations because it says do not judge according to outward appearances, and we are not permitted to judge a person's heart.

Paul spoke of the ministry of death which was written on stones (living by Law) verses the ministry of righteousness. The ministry of righteousness or righteous judgment is the announcement of how right we are with God. It is how He set everything right. So people may have unhealthy beliefs, or self-destructive behaviors but they are still in right standing as children of God living before the face of their Father's love. That means while we cannot judge the outward, we can rest our hearts on the truth that love is the hidden unexperienced truth in that situation or person's life. If they can't see it, you can.

Before long, coincidences and reinforcements of what you are looking for will appear on a regular basis. So in order to escape seeing what you have always seen, you'll need to choose to see something else until it becomes second nature.

Which leads me to another very important heart truth…

Heart Truth 11—The Heart Can't Tell the Difference Between Real and Imagined.

My friend Jen told me this beautiful story. On her son Joshua's second birthday, he broke his leg and came down with hand, foot, and mouth disease at the same time. With a 105 degree fever for two weeks, and painful rashes on his hands, feet and mouth, all he could do was sit perfectly still in her arms. Even a tiny movement hurt him terribly.

So they watched "Angels in the Outfield." When they finished that video, he wanted to watch it again. And again. And again. Little Joshua fell in love with it! In fact, the only thing they did for those two weeks was to watch "Angels in the Outfield" all day, every day. He was intently focused on every detail after he understood the basic story. He noticed all the nuances.

After two weeks of not moving at all, his fever broke, his leg was healed, and guess what he wanted to do? He wanted to play baseball for the first time. So she bought him a small plastic bat and ball and went outside to pitch to him, thinking she would be teaching him how to hold the bat, how to hit the ball and how to play baseball.

She was wrong. First pitch, he hit it hard and long! Second pitch, he did it again. Third pitch, again a two-year-old-sized home run. He never missed a hit.

In those two weeks of intently observing the video, he loved it so much that he visualized hitting the ball so many hundreds of times, that when he actually held the bat in his hand for the first time, he was already a professional in his own mind. And he swung like he knew what he was doing because he did.

Of course, I laughed when she said he also learned how to imitate spiting chewing tobacco like the pitcher in the movie!

The endeared images impressed upon our hearts are powerful tools because our hearts don't know the difference between the real and the imagined pictures!

"I Can Only Imagine" Exercise
Purpose: to fix our heart's imagination on that through which *dunamis*-power will flow

Einstein said, "The true sign of intelligence is not knowledge but imagination." Be a genius and use the same method that God and other geniuses do.

Let me share with you a powerful simple secret to using the imagination. When I say imagine, I don't even necessarily mean that you always imagine with your eyes closed. It's ok to close your eyes, but I have found it to be more effective to imagine with my eyes wide open. By seeing yourself in the context of real life and at the same time with your "mind's eye" (I call it your heart's eyes) seeing what you need/want, it will cause your heart to be more readily impacted with a powerful image.

In other words, let's say one of my dreams is to build hundreds of wells in leper villages in India. Instead of closing my eyes and trying to create a picture, which some aren't as skilled at doing, it would be better to look at a photograph of a leper village and with your heart's eyes, imagine them smiling at you and you handing them buckets of water. It creates a more life-like, vivid image this way. Your heart is more likely to lower its "guard" like this.

While doing your NOW exercise, finish by imagining a new scenario in as much detail as possible. What does it look like? What things are you doing? Where are you? How much money do you have in the bank? What do you feel like? How will you be helping others?

Paint the picture as real and vivid. Remember, your heart can't tell the difference between what is real or imagined when you are feeding it pictures that you love and grow to believe. Feel the image, don't just see it.

Instead of starting with your big dream which may require many mini steps and possibly a longer period of time, start with something small, just so you can see the power of this principle. Let's say you want a pair of movie tickets given to you or you want to develop a new good habit. Or maybe you need to see yourself as a successful insurance salesman.

Use the same principles... *see* it, *ask* for it, *love* it, *trust* the *dunamis*-power of love will take that image and bring it to pass. Hold your heart steady in that state or keep bringing it back to that state as you wait for things to change. Then, (this is very important) start looking, noticing, watching for it to happen.

Events may line up to benefit you, or it may mean you change and begin to take action that you never dreamed possible before. It can be both. So...

Every Night Write Down In Your Journal Any Evidence that You Saw that Day of Your Desire/Belief Coming True. *I cannot overemphasize how important this part of the exercise is for you.* This trains your heart to perceive the new desire/belief happening. The more you pay attention to it, the more you will find evidence.

The Power of Radical Hope: Embody the Future Now

"Everything that is done in the world is done by hope." –Martin Luther

His promises are already yes and amen and He has invited us to enjoy life. His world is filled with himself and His abundance so we can ask whatever we need, opening the door wide open. So what is the problem? The problem is that we don't know HOW TO RECEIVE our dream.

But let patience have its perfect work, that you may be perfect and complete, lacking nothing. If any of you lacks wisdom, let him ask of God, who gives to all, liberally and without reproach, and it will be given to him. But let him ask in faith, with no doubting, for he who doubts is like a wave of the sea driven and tossed by the wind. For let not that man suppose that he will receive anything from the Lord. (James 1:4-7)

The problem is not that the Lord isn't giving it. It is already invisibly and intentionally given. Every good and perfect gift continues to flow from Him as if it were a steady invisible stream of His life-giving presence. It means that when our hearts are patient or enduring in heart-faith, we are able to easily receive. Often, though, it's as if we are saying, *"He loves me, He loves me not"*, which cause us to struggle to receive.

The word for *receive* is *lambano*, which means to "actively take something". It's similar to my daughter asking me for one hundred dollars and me pulling it out of my wallet and stretching it out toward her, yet she is still waiting for it. I've already said yes and it now belongs to her, but she isn't *taking* it as if it belongs to her. Of course, in real life I've never had that problem with my kids.

We know how to ask but we don't really know how to *receive* because we have for so long not understood the way the heart works. I remember understanding the meaning of the word but not knowing practically what it really meant to receive.

What is Hope?

Have you embraced a false definition of hope? When you say "I hope so" do you mean "I wish"? Wishing is mere fancy, a whisper of desire with no substance. It has nothing to do with real Biblical transformational Beyond Your Wildest Dreams hope.

The dictionary definition of hope is this: *the feeling that what is wanted can be had or that events will turn out for the best.*

Hope is a feeling, not a wish. Biblical hope is the *belief* AND the *feeling* that what I desire is certain. It is as if I feel I possess it *now*! You are a feeling person. Though there is a difference between feelings and emotions, for our purposes I am using them interchangeably.

John says, "*May you prosper and be in health even as your soul prospers.*" As your soul—the realm of feeling in the body—prospers, it works its way outward into every area of life, from our health to our finances and to situations in life. So *receiving* is the feeling in the heart of *certainty* that what I have asked is already mine, *now*. Mark 11:24 says, **"Therefore I say to you, whatever things you ask when you pray, believe that** *you receive them, and you will have them."*

Don't miss this important truth: You are the first one to bring it from the invisible to the visible THROUGH your life when you FEEL it as if it is true now; at that point you are already beginning to manifest the miracle.

Become in yourself the change that you want to see manifested in your life or in the world. Feel it to be true now. Own it. Possess it.

Heart Truth 12—The Heart Is the Epicenter of Emotions.

Scholars have long taught that the heart is also the seat of the emotions. These emotions can be influenced by the outward, the information coming from the soul. Or the heart can be influenced by the spirit, which is the inner energy of God. Either way, beliefs in the heart are rooted in information or revelation combined with emotion. All you have to do is try to change a belief and you will realize how emotions are tied to it. Something doesn't "feel" true.

The truth is that *feelings are the greatest indicator of what we really believe.* We should not live by every feeling but they do tell us what we are believing. They can be the red signal light on the dashboard of our lives telling us something is wrong. Peace and joy can be our norm.

On the other hand, if you believe that a car is about to hit you as you step off a sidewalk, then before you have a chance to think, a healthy belief will cause you to jump back instantly. The belief produced instantaneous adrenaline and warned you to jump, but it started with a belief.

So for all of us, the problem is not our ability to believe. The problem is that there is already a contradictory belief that your unguarded heart accepted. That contradictory belief has a feeling attached to it. So in order to change the belief, you must change the feeling. The other belief is what "feels" true. Every limiting belief has a feeling associated with it and if it doesn't coincide with peace, goodness and joy then it isn't the wisdom of God.

Or to say it another way, any belief that isn't in harmony with love isn't true. Paul said to speak the truth in love, therefore, truth without love isn't truth. It is a lie. God is love. Jesus is the Truth. Truth and Love are inseparable. That is why James said (James 4:3), *"You ask and do not receive, because you ask amiss, that you may spend it on your pleasures."* The context is that they were not receiving because they wanted the answers to their prayers to harm others; it was a contradiction to love.

I was taught not to live by our feelings, but they were only partially right. Don't live by feelings of fear, doubt, and jealousy. Love, though, is not only an attitude and an action, it is a feeling. Joy is a feeling. Peace is not only a realm but a feeling of tranquility and the absence of internal conflict. Godly emotions/feelings are part and parcel of the place from which we are to live. Live from love, peace and joy.

Love is the source of all good feelings. Galatians 5:22-24 says, "But the fruit of the Spirit is love, joy, peace, patience, kindness, goodness, faith, gentleness, self-control." In this list, love is not one among many, it is the fountainhead from which the others flow. Notice how Paul also said in 1 Cor. 13 that *love is patient and love is kind*. So the patience and kindness we just read in

Galatians are actually expressions of love. Love is the source for it all!

Every healthy emotion and character trait flows out of love. Donald Grey Barnhouse said, "Joy is love singing, peace is love resting, patience is love enduring, kindness is love's truth, goodness is love's character, faithfulness is love's habit, gentleness is love's self-forgetfulness, self-control is (love) being the reins."

So the more we learn to harness love, the more we can harness the power of love to change how we feel.

Then what is hope? Hope is love's certainty. The transformation of our hearts into love is what drives out false beliefs and the feelings attached to them. We mistakenly think that in order to change the old feeling, we need to fight it, resist it, pluck it out, tear it down, or cast it out. But perfect love casts out all fear. All that is needed is to fill yourself with love and the by-product is that it dissolves the negative feelings attached to old beliefs.

Hope is the feeling that will wash out the contradictions to your dream. Filling your heart with hope is one of the most powerful tools for fulfilling your dreams!

Hope is the feeling that what is wanted and promised is already mine. Notice how love is the reason that hope doesn't disappoint. Romans 5:5 says, *"Now hope does not disappoint because the love of God has been poured out in our hearts by the Holy Spirit who was given to us."* Knowing you are loved, and loving your dream, gives you the right to hope; it drives out hopelessness. When your dream is as if it is present tense, even though you know it is not physically in your possession yet, you will not be disappointed.

Faith is the substance of things *hoped* for, the evidence of things unseen. Let me read that sentence backward and reword it: faith is evidence that you are seeing the unseen. It is the foundation of feeling confident now of things expected.

"But what if I get my hopes up and it doesn't happen?" But what if it *does*? Often times when we are disappointed by something it is because we are trying to control the process. In other words, we believe that God wants to give us a new job. Then we imagine it so, we see ourselves enjoying the new job, going out to lunch with the new friends and finishing projects. But then we tell God HOW to do it by saying that it has to happen a certain way, or it must unfold exactly like we want. As soon as we start trying to control the process we are doing nothing more than using Him as our heavenly Bellhop.

Instead of using God, trust Him, trust the power of love through your heart. Let go of control of HOW it will come to pass, or how He will arrange the new job. Or to say it another way, let go of how the universe will shift for your benefit and watch how it does!

Authenticity goes beyond mental assent to the truth. Authenticity is the whole being coming into alignment with the truth. That means if we think we believe something but we don't feel it, then it hasn't fully reached our hearts yet. Mark 11:24 says, ***"Therefore I say to you, whatever things you ask when you pray, believe that you receive them, and you will have them."***

Let me say it again. I'm not teaching you a "faith movement" principle, or "name-it-and-claim-it" idea or a magic trick for the universe. This is how your heart works! **You are the first one to bring it from the invisible to the visible THROUGH your**

life. When you FEEL it as if it is true *now* you are already manifesting the miracle. *Become* the change within yourself that you want to see manifested in your life or in the world. *Feel* it to be true *now*. Own it. Possess it.

Let me use sales again as an example. It is one thing to imagine yourself making more sales than you did last year and seeing yourself loving your product and your clients. It is another to feel it to be true now, to feel like the top producer in your company. It is powerful to begin feeling as if the product is sold before it sells. At that point there is an otherworldly power that is at work beyond confidence. It is the power of hope where a miracle is manifesting THROUGH you. It will be no surprise to you when you make the sale over and over again and become the top producer because it was your internal norm before it was your external experience.

Go With the Flow of Life or Resist It?

This brings up some important questions. Am I to go with the flow of life, as some teach, or do I resist it with prayer and action as if life were a battle I need to win?

Let me tweak each of these. Much of our energy is spent trying to resist life, as if it were some evil overall strategy trying to crush our dreams. Can I share something with you? God is for you, therefore nothing can be ultimately against you. That means life is for you. Don't waste the attention of your heart about things that you cannot control and that are already in the past. The secret of letting go is knowing that not even God changes the past. Learn to accept it as is, and as gone.

In this way life unfolds new today with new lessons and new opportunities. Playwright John Patrick Shanley once said, "I picture each day as if it were a happy dog looking at me. I may not be in the mood, but the dog always wants to play. Trust the dog."

I often counsel people who are frustrated because they are praying "harder" than ever, which translates as they are begging God and blaming Him the longer they don't get an answer. Then of course, the volume increases, not because of passion or love, but out of trying to exercise some kind of "authority" out of anger.

Did you ever notice the prayer life of Jesus? Jesus *never* prayed to the Father one time to ask for the healing of someone. He never asked the Father to walk on water, nor did He ask the Father to multiply bread. He did not even ask the Father to raise Him from the dead. Not once. He trusted. He thanked the Father as if it were already his. He already knew what the will of God was. So what did He do? He exercised the authority that He already possessed.

I believe in prayer but what you will discover is that bringing your heart into the equation means that many times you won't have to pray at all. That may sound unusual but I realized that Jesus spent time with His Father for communion, and out of His expanded heart connection miracles happened and situations worked for His benefit. The Bible says that He "grew in favor". He already had favor but out of communion in His heart with the Father He grew INTO experiencing it more and more and stuff just "happened".

Some people think that Jesus first saw specific people, opportunities or circumstances that the Father showed Him before he actually ministered to them. That absolutely can happen for us but it mostly works the other way. What did Jesus

ALWAYS see the Father doing? Healing the sick, cleansing the lepers, forgiving sin. Jesus *saw* it first, *believed* it, *felt* its truth and the invisible beliefs set things in motion resulting in opportunities which emerged all around him.

My friend Dwayne pursued healing the sick through this method and after a while he started experiencing it everywhere he went. It wasn't just that he noticed it more (which he did), but something unusual started to happen. Strangers who knew nothing about his love of healing would open up out of the blue and start telling him where they had pain in their body. His heart belief attracted opportunities to him because there is incredible dream convergence when invisible heart beliefs attract answers and situations into our lives. What is your internal norm attracting outwardly?

There is a saying in carpentry that you measure twice and cut once. But when it comes to loving and living your dream, I've learned to *believe twice and pray once*. I believe the truth, pray once and then continue to abide in the feeling of hope. Remember that life is like a dog wagging it's tail. Feel the joy, trust the dog and play!

The Certainty of Hope

But how can you be so certain? 1 Peter 1:3 tells us something very important about hope: *"Blessed be the God and Father of our Lord Jesus Christ, who according to His abundant mercy has begotten us again to a living hope through the resurrection of Jesus Christ from the dead…"* (ESV).

Hope is embodied in the resurrected Christ. Did the Father promise to raise Jesus from the dead? Yes. Did the Son trust the Father? Yes. In fact, what do you think He was doing for three days in Hades? Here is part of the very first sermon preached of the Gospel after the resurrection. Peter quotes David in describing what Jesus was doing in Hades:

> *But God raised Him up again, putting an end to the agony of death since it was impossible for Him to be held in its power. For David says **of Him**, 'I **saw** the Lord **always** in My presence, for **He** is at my right hand, **so that I will not be shaken**. Therefore **My heart was glad and My tongue exulted**; moreover, My flesh also will live in **hope because You will not abandon My soul** to Hades, nor allow Your Holy One to undergo decay. 'You have made known to Me **the ways of life**; You will make Me full of gladness with Your presence.'* (Acts 2:24-28)

With joy (emotion, as if it were already completed), patience (three days in Hades), certainty of expectation (the feeling of hope) and faith (steady confidence in who the Father is), Jesus meditated (saw and imagined) and set the image of the Father and the resurrection before His heart until... the Father raised Jesus from the dead!

"Your Feeler" Exercise:

1. Using the NOW exercise, or Breath Prayer, **get your awareness into the present with God.**

2. What is your desire or the next step in your dream? Is it marriage to the right person for you? Is it a car for

your teenager? Is it working somewhere that uses all your gifts and talents to the fullest? Is it making a certain income each week to fund you while freeing you to travel? Is it leading worship in a church or is it becoming a writer of children's books? *Whatever you want to focus on, write down again ALL the things you love about that dream.*

3. Visualize it being fulfilled in as much detail as possible.

Go into the future in your imagination and hear someone congratulating you for reaching your goals and fulfilling your dream. See yourself living it to the fullest in every detail. Why do you think God spoke to Abraham by showing him the stars and telling him that his seed would be more numerous than the stars? He was activating Abraham's imagination about the future. Visualize it with your eyes wide open, with your "mind's eye", and in the environment you are in right now.

4. What would it FEEL like to be walking out that dream?

You have permission to allow yourself to feel as if it were already fulfilled. As you are visualizing/meditating your dream being fulfilled and people congratulating you, what would that feel like? Embrace that feeling. In your imagination, look up to heaven and thank God for giving you the desires of your heart!

For instance, if your dream over the next 5 months is to lose 50 pounds, start by allowing your heart to love *that* dream. Remember how God loves that dream. Think about how good you will feel. Love the current you and the future picture of you 50 pounds lighter. Love the feeling of being lighter. *Feel thinner.* Love the things that you will do differently. Love, love, love.

By doing so, you are establishing hope in your heart and you become the one bringing the invisible into the visible by allowing yourself to embody the future in the now. You are the conduit from the spiritual into the physical!

5. Do you feel as if there is a contradictory belief

resisting this in your heart? Well, of course there probably is. We all deal with them. But, remember it is easy to believe and God is the Author of your faith working to convince you. The new belief plus the new emotion of hope will displace the negative emotion associated with the limiting belief.

1. Take a moment and be thankful for love. Drink it in for a few minutes.

2. Now take out your journal again and ask yourself these questions:

> A. Can I know with 100% absolute certainty that this negative/limiting belief I have is true? Are these things really holding me back?
>
> Why might it not be true? Write down any and everything that comes to mind.
>
> B. Is it at all possible that there are other scriptures or understandings of God that I have not considered or been made aware of? Is it possible that God may want to change this belief? Yes or no?

3. Next, write down the opposite of that negative belief.

4. Once you write that positively do a "heart-belief buster". This means use your journal to write down in short ideas and statements any thoughts that come to you when you say that statement positively. It may take 10 minutes to allow all the thoughts, positive and negative, to come out of the darkness of your heart into the light. Don't judge them, just write... and your perspective will softly change.

By itself, simply bringing them to the light will often dispel the negative beliefs.

5. What would my life look like if this positive belief was true? Write it down.

6. Prayer: "Father I want to acknowledge every good thing that is in me by Christ Jesus and every good thing about You. Since I need this new belief established in my heart, supply faith to me with evidences, encouragement and signs that it is true."

7. Now sit in His presence in the present with any residual negative emotions and just let them pass through you. Ask God to cleanse your heart with His life, love and light. Rest in that moment like you are simply watching it happen until you sense release and peace.

Conclusion: What Now?

The vision must be followed by the venture. It is not enough to stare up the steps - we must step up the stairs. -Vance Havner

What now? Step up the stairs! You have been on a journey through this book. If you have been doing the exercises, you should be able to look back and already see an emerging confidence, a healthier self-image, your dream coming to the surface and a strategy for bringing a stage of your dream to pass.

Of course, if your dream is to be a surgeon, it may be time to apply to medical school. If your dream is to have a ministry of some kind, then you may need to learn some practical skills, or talk to that Prison Ministry leader. Out of authenticity into loving who you are, loving what you want and becoming love in your life, you will see miracles of open doors, provision and strategic relationships begin to happen. So go dream your dream, go apply for that job, make plans to move to that city, whatever it is, you take the steps. Dreams are not passive! Go Beyond Your Wildest Dreams!

But isn't there something else practical I should be doing?

Heart Truth 13—The Heart Is Established by Grace through Patience.

Hebrews 13:9, ***Do not be carried about with various and strange doctrines. For it is good that <u>the heart be established by grace</u>...*** " The heart is to be established in the context of grace. That is what this whole book is trying to help you experience.

Remember in the last chapter you learned that hope is not just a promise, but it is a feeling resulting from it? Notice how hope is associated with joy and patiently staying in that state of being: Romans 12:12, *"rejoicing in hope, patient in tribulation, continuing steadfastly in prayer..."* The Bible also says that hope (the feeling connected to an expectation) is patient until we see with our natural eyes what we are seeing with the eyes of our heart. The new belief or dream seed in your heart takes time to grow roots. Keep watering it with faith, hope and love.

Be patient throughout your journey. It will unfold as it unfolds. You will find that some portions happen very quickly, while others seem like a molasses clock in a cartoon dream. If there is something that needs to change along the way, you will bump into that limiting belief, face it with the power of love and take another leap forward.

Don't quit your day job, though. See this as a process. There may be periods of transition in your life where you are selling insurance and becoming a dance professional at the same time. Keep applying the principle, revisiting the processes and you will know when to let go of one job to fully embrace the other. Remember your identity isn't in what you do, or don't do, it is in what God says about you. Working a job that isn't your dream, is just a stepping stone, especially if you will love people in the "in-between" position.

Patience is not about holding to your dream with claw marks and death grips. It is more about staying present in the moment where all strength is found. Don't be so focused on the end result that you miss the life right in front of you. You are needed now. The present is the only moment there is. Love now.

Role-Play Your Dream

James 1:22-24, *"But be doers of the word, and not hearers only, deceiving yourselves. For if anyone is a hearer of the word and not a doer, he is like a man observing his natural face in a mirror; for he observes himself, goes away, and immediately forgets what kind of man he was."*

The Greek word for "doer" means a doer, a performer, a poet. What does a Method Actor do with a script? He doesn't just read the lines by rote memory. No, he **feels** the character and then plays the character. He puts the appropriate emotion behind it. Some are afraid of completely giving themselves to the truth of who they are and what they want for fear that they may be hypocritical if they don't "feel it" yet. But you aren't pretending to be something or someone that's not true. You are embracing things about you that *God* says are true.

So it may mean that you go so far as to even role-play your dream.

- Practice overcoming objections to your product with the feeling of confidence as if you were sitting in front of them right now.
- Patiently see yourself being proposed to by the man of your dreams. Take a ring and put it on your finger as you joyfully imagine and practice saying yes now.
- Or set your schedule just like you are going to work each day as if you already had the job. Wake up and work at home as if you had a new work schedule for your dream job.
- Each time you make a deposit at the bank, take it in your hands, feel the paper and imagine you are excitedly depositing $10,000 checks.

- When I was younger, one of the things I learned about teaching is that if I didn't have an opportunity, I would just prayerfully prepare a message first, imagine myself preaching it to others passionately and then watch as doors would suddenly open for me to share it.

That is why James says, ***"Don't look at yourself in the mirror of the Word, where God has told you who you are, and then walk away and forget who you are."*** Continue to see and feel the truth of yourself and your dream!

Steadfastly, immovably, unshakably, continually, patiently FEEL the LOVE by..

- being in the present tense and loving your worthy self and valuable life now.
- accessing your inner awesome and being the person you were created to be!
- changing any Global God-Belief that is inaccurate and limiting your life.
- trusting the endless supply created for you from an abundant universe.
- bringing goals and dreams to the surface of your heart and saying them out loud daily.
- imagining what you want vividly with your eyes wide open.
- setting the intentions of your heart like a thermostat.
- living in hope as if it is already here.

Become the change that you want to see until you see it happening in your life! As your heart transforms, so will you and the world around you.

Create Massive Action

Next, create massive action many times more than the results that you want to achieve. Paul said *those who sow a little will reap a little, but those who sow much will reap much.* If you dream of being the top sales-person then make more calls than any other sales person in the company. If you want to write a blog that is read world-wide then cast your net bigger wider. Even Jesus said good seed can fall on bad soil, so sow more good seed than anyone else if you want to get results beyond your wildest dreams.

Love is the energy for this massive action. When you have a beautiful dream and you are filled with hope, that feeling is a continual impetus for excellence.

This is vitally important. Don't play safe and small! Average sowing is not going to bring success. Sow extensively and continually into your field of endeavor into the things that will give you the most important results!

Over the years I watched many think that since our relationship with God isn't based on "work" at all, that *nothing* in life requires work. But there is a dignity in working hard and sowing massively for a beautiful purpose and dream.

Paul, the premier grace preacher said, *"But by the [remarkable] grace of God I am what I am, and His grace toward me was not without effect. In fact, I worked harder than all of the apostles, though it was not I, but the grace of God [His unmerited favor and blessing which was] with me"* (1 Cor. 15:10, AMP). By knowing who you are and what is in you by the grace of God, you are empowered to work harder and smarter to achieve more than others.

Divest yourself of excuses. Steward your heart and actions to accomplish your dreams. As Art Leazer, president of The Leazer Group, Inc. says, "You can make excuses, or you can make money, but you can't do both!" You can come up with all kinds of reasons why you can't achieve your dreams, or you can give up excuses and just do it! Excuses are heart noise. Ignore them. What are you waiting for? Now you have the tools!

Listen To Your Intuitive Heart

Actor Sissy Spacek said, "Everyone has an inner voice; you just have to listen to it and trust it in order to be led by it. I did that and it gave me the ability to live a life that's true to who I am." All the direction you need for your next step is in the slight impulses and insights your heart is speaking. Don't ignore them... follow their lead. Highly value their importance.

Remember fear is not a direction. It is a deception. God doesn't lead your heart with fear, but with wisdom. Fear means I believe there is no love within the unknown future.

I've done counseling/discipleship for many years with drug addicts, struggling couples and dissatisfied businessmen. One of the common threads I've noticed is that everyone really already knows what they need to do about a situation because it was already in their heart. They just needed someone to help them see it clearly. What YOU need to know for your next step is already there, even if you need someone to help you get to it. Listen to it.

Where Do You Go From Here?

Where do you go from here? Dream your dream. Do what others only wish for. You only have one life to live. Love that life, love your dream, and love people along the way, and you will be amazed at the stories you will have to pass down to your grandchildren. That's how you live Beyond Your Wildest Dreams.

What is your next step? What does your intuition say? Write down the next action you will take:

Want Personalized Coaching?

With years of personal experience and professional coaching, we have a variety of packages available to help you if you want to develop a personalized plan.

I believe in the value of coaching because I regularly receive coaching for myself, and I've witnessed its effectiveness in those I help.

Our coaching can be done through phone, Skype or similar formats.

Let us help guide you through discovering and implementing your heart's desires.

Please contact us at www.ANewDayDawning.com or AwesomeAmazingYou@gmail.com

Blessings to you!
Dr Chuck Crisco